THE GOSPEL OF PEACE

By Father John J. Hugo

WITH DRAWINGS BY FATHER E. M. CATICH AND A. DE BETHUNE

PRIVATELY PRINTED

LORETO PUBLICATIONS
FITZWILLIAM NEW HAMPSHIRE
AD 2018

NIHIL OBSTAT

ARTHUR J. SCANLAN, S.T.D.
Censor Librorum

IMPRIMATUR

✠FRANCIS J. SPELLMAN, D.D.
Archbishop, New York
New York, August 15, 1944

Re-published by Loreto Publications - 2018
ISBN 978-1-62292-132-4

Cover design by Michael Hamilton

Cover art: *Sermon on The Mount* by Carl Heinrich Bloch

Loreto Publications
P. O. Box 603
Fitzwilliam, NH 03447
603-239-6671
www.LoretoPubs.org

Printed and Bound in the United States

**"How beautiful are the feet
of those who preach
The Gospel of Peace;
Of those who bring glad tidings
of good things!"**

—St. Paul (Rom. 10, 15).

COME·FOLLOW·ME

LORETO PUBLICATIONS FORWORD

The twentieth century has been called by many the "bloodiest of centuries," "the American Century," and most recently by Jewish writer Yuri Slezkine, "The Jewish Century." All three nicknames have many cogent arguments to support their use, but no matter what history calls it, there is no doubt that it has been a time of great moral, spiritual, and political ferment. Just two of its many wars have already earned the name of World War. To the Catholic there is always only one war, and it will be waged constantly from that terrible day in the Garden of Eden until that awesome day of the Second Coming of Our Blessed Lord and Savior Jesus Christ our King. The war is always and everwhere between the Kingdom of Christ and that of the Prince of this World.

It is Catholic priests who are so often found in the front lines of this perpetual battle, and even such an anti-catholic nation as the USA has produced in this bloody century some couragous and holy priests who have in one way or another "fought the good fight" against evil and for the salvation of souls. It is important for us as Catholic Americans to remember these men and to honor their sacrifices. Priests like Fr. Charles Coughlin, Bishop Fulton Sheen, Fr. Leonard Feeney, and the two to whom Loreto dedicates this publication, Fr. Onesimus Lacouture (the inspiration of it) and Fr. John Hugo (the author of it), should be models of inspiration for us, as they were for countless souls during their lifetimes.

The Holy Spirit blows where He will, and He inspires those faithful who wish to live a Christ-like life, toward many different means of service to Christ the King. For Father Lacouture and Fr. Hugo and other American and Canadian priests, their method of service was *The Retreat.* The preceding words are in italics because that is how those disciples of Fr. Onesimus most affected by his spiritual direction affectionately termed it. They also called it simply *The Doctrine*, in much the same way that the disciples of Father Feeney always spoke of *extra ecclesiam nulla salus*, as *The Dogma* or referred to the first fourteen verses of St. John's Gospel as *The Center Prayer* (the Last Gospel of the Mass which all of Father's disciples could recite from memory in Latin and English).

The Retreat, as it was called is nothing more nor less than the Spiritual Excercises of Saint Ignatius. But these retreats given by Fr. Lacouture were, as the saying goes "the real deal." They were given as St. Ignatius intended, for the proper length of time and according to the true Ignatian spirit. Father Lacouture was a Jesuit, as was Father Feeney. In fact, Fr. Lacouture and Fr. Feeney were both trained at St. Andrews-on-the-Hudson; Fr. Onesimus preceeding Fr. Feeney by about fifteen years. What made the retreats that Fr. Lacouture gave very special were two things: 1) he only gave them to priests (over 6000 priests in a few years time took his retreat) and 2) he was a masterful spiritual director and doctor of souls.

Father Lacouture, like all of the priests mentioned above, ran into opposition because of the spectacular results he achieved for the building up of the Kingdom of Christ. In his case, the retreats were stopped dead in their tracks after a few years by his superiors, and he was internally exiled and forbidden to give any more retreats. But he had disciples, many disciples, because of the efficacy of his work. In the USA his work was continued by many priests, most famously by Fr. John Hugo who gave the retreats until the time of his death in 1985. Notably, the retreats in the USA were given primarily to the laity, and one of the groups of laity who not only attended these retreats (often many times) but who credit the retreats as being a prominent source, if not the driving motivation of their organization, was the Catholic Worker Movement founded by Peter Maurin and Dorothy Day. Father Hugo was her spiritual director and she took the retreat over twenty times during her life. (Please see the appendix for her brief eulogy of Fr. Lacouture upon his death in 1951.)

If, as the scriptues say "by their fruits you shall know them," one may judge Father Lacouture's work by the tremendous impact he had on the spiritual lives of thousands of priests in Canada and the USA and the extended effect upon the laity who were inspired and affected by the lives of those priests.

The influence that Fr. Lacouture excercised on priests in Quebec was legendary, so legendary in fact that his disciples received a nickname of opprobrium similar to the term *Jesuites* that was hurled at the disciples of St. Ignatius or *Feeneyites* that was cast at the Slaves of the Immaculate Heart of Mary, the order that was founded by Fr. Feeney. The general movement toward true Ignatian spirituality on the part of the priests who were spiritually recharged by these retreats was called *Lacouturisme*. And, like all truly Catholic movements, it was opposed vigorously by the world and by worldlings, both inside and outside of the Church. Neither he, nor his retreats, nor the books that sprang from his retreats were ever officially censured in any way by the Church. He was just asked, (and forced) to "go away," like Our Lord was asked to depart by the Gerasenes.

Father Lacouture's faithful disciple, Fr. John Hugo, wrote three books relative to *The Retreat*. *The Gospel of Peace* is the one I call "the fruit." The second is titled *A Sign of Contradiction* and I call that one "the polemic," since it defends Fr. Lacouture and *The Retreat*. The third was *Applied Christianity*, which I call "the doctrine" since it is the notes of the retreats reflecting the doctrine of Jesus Christ according to St. Ignatius and his spiritual descendants. So that Fr. Lacouture and Fr. Hugo and the work that they did may be better known and appreciated, Loreto Publications will soon publish the other two books.

Like St. Ignatius and Fr. Feeney who both threw down the gauntlet, so to speak, to the world of their day, Fr. Hugo in this book throws down the challenge of the Gospel of Peace of Jesus Christ to the most blood-soaked century in history. It is a hard saying and who can take it. We feel it is just what the world needs today at a moment when worldwide war may break out once again without warning.

Loreto Publications
The Feast of Saint Hermengild 2018

Table of Contents

INTRODUCTORY

I. Supernatural Morality

Most Catholics know something of the *ethical* principles that determine the justice of *war*. Unfortunately, there is not such general knowledge of the *theological* truths that fix the conditions for attaining true *peace*. Often those who know about St. Thomas's requirements for a just war cannot speak so readily about his doctrine of peace. This means that they form their judgments on war according to the rules of natural ethics, leaving out of account the higher principles that govern supernatural life and activity. As a consequence, they easily fall into the *doctrinal error* of regarding armed force (so long as it is used in a just cause, which a patriot never has difficulty in finding) as a proportionate and at times necessary means for securing peace.

There are other false notions that arise from the preoccupation with merely ethical norms. It is inferred, for example, that the Gospel teaching is irrelevant to the problem of war. This problem (so it is held) must be solved by principles of reason rather than by the truths of faith. Such indeed *must* be the conclusion, sometimes tacit, at other times boldly asserted, that comes of failure to consider the bearings of the Gospel on the use of force. From the circumstance that reason alone is in fact so commonly considered sufficient to cope with this matter, it is then concluded that this must be so, and is rightfully so, and that Revelation therefore need not be consulted nor its truths and sanctions called upon to intervene. The supernatural principles of Christ are considered not to apply; conviction and conduct should be based on the teachings of natural ethics. The Gospel is not pertinent, and the whole problem is one of natural law.

In this way Catholics frequently come to take their ideas concerning war exclusively from natural law, ethics, the truths of reason. If they do not in so many words throw out the Gospel, they at least reason as though the Gospel did not exist.

They leave to one side all specifically Christian principles, Revelation, the evangelic law.

Another inadmissible idea which originates in the same false emphasis is the belief that the spirit and laws of the Gospel are not opposed to war; that the Gospel, indeed, is rather indifferent to the whole matter; and that we can therefore make no effective protest against war on the basis of the teachings of Jesus. It is not without significance in this regard that the pacifist is frequently regarded by Catholics as acting out of sentimentality or humanitarianism rather than from pure and authentic religious motives. Hence it is customary to cast slurs on the pacifist's profession of Christianity, calling it weak, or false, or heterodox. In other words, it is not believed that one can make a protest against war on the basis of the Gospels; it is therefore denied that a Catholic can embrace pacifism. So it comes about frequently that if a follower of the Prince of Peace opposes war, he is likely to find that his orthodoxy is suspected by devotees of Mars.

Against such views it must be asserted that no problem may be solved without Christ. That is, no problem can be solved satisfactorily by principles of natural law *alone* and without taking into account the loftier teachings of the Gospel. Nor may such a solution even be attempted. It is God's eternal design to "re-establish *all things* in Christ." (1) No one may change that order. Christ is henceforth to "be all and in all." (2) Human actions therefore have value and significance only to the extent that they are "in Christ Jesus." "As therefore ye have received Christ the Lord, *walk ye in Him; rooted and built up in Him. . . .*" (3) The quality in good works which makes them acceptable to God is, not their conformity with the mere natural standards of morality and goodness, but the fact that they are performed *in union with Jesus Christ*. "Without Him let nothing seem comely to you," wrote St. Ignatius of Antioch. And St. Bernard shows how far we are to carry this principle: "If you write, your composition has no charms for

---

(1) Eph. 1, 10.
(2) Col. 3, 11.
(3) Col. 2, 6.

me unless I read therein the name of Jesus. If you discourse or converse, I find no pleasure in your words unless I hear there the name of Jesus." (4) The knowledge and grace of Christ transform all things: "If then any man is in Christ, he is *a new creature*: the former things have passed away; behold, they are made new!" (5)

We act *in Christ Jesus* when our principles, dispositions and motives are those of Jesus, when our actions are guided by the truths which He taught, impelled by the energy of divine grace, motivated by the love of God which He infuses into our souls. In a word, to act *in Christ* means that we are so filled with His spirit, His doctrine, His life, that we are able to say with the Apostle: "I live, now not I, but Christ liveth in me." (6)

We who have received the Gospel of Jesus, the example of His life, and the abundance of His grace are no longer free to act except *in union with Him.*

If this is true of all things, it is so particularly of peace, for peace is in a special way the gift of God. "Grace be with you, mercy, *and peace from God the Father,* and *from Jesus Christ,* the Son of the Father; in truth and charity." (7) The Gospel is by no means irrelevant to the problem of peace. It is not to be forgotten that the peculiar message and teaching of Jesus was called "the Gospel *of Peace.*" (8) We must discuss and settle the problem of war, not by the principles of Aristotle alone, however commendable these may be in their own order. We must speak and act and think in Christ Jesus. If it is permissible to study the principles of natural ethics *in themselves,* and apart from the rules of conduct given in the Gospel, this is only for the sake of orderly and logical procedure in systematizing knowledge. *In practice,* however—that is, in regulating our actual conduct—we may never disregard the Gospel, but must ever and in all things seek to act in accordance with its

---

(4) Quoted from Ailbe J. Luddy, Life and Teaching of St. Bernard, p. 93. (Dublin: M. H. Gill, 1937.)
(5) II Cor. 5, 17.
(6) Gal. 2, 20.
(7) II St. John, 1, 3.
(8) Eph. 6, 15.

spirit and teaching. "Be deaf therefore when anyone speaks to you apart from Jesus Christ. . . ." (9)

Necessary as it is to know something of the natural principles that determine the justice of war, it is far more necessary to know and to apply the supernatural truths that reveal the conditions for obtaining true peace. Not least, indeed, among the motives for studying the rights and duties of natural law is the need to know the manner in which nature has been elevated and transformed by grace. For as iron is transformed by fire, while still remaining iron, so is nature transformed by grace. Certain persons, overzealous for nature while neglecting the truths of the supernatural order, are fond of repeating the theological axiom, "Grace perfects nature and does not destroy it." But is it not precisely the point of this axiom that nature is still perfectible, and therefore of itself imperfect and incomplete?

If St. Thomas's authority can be cited to support the view that war may in certain circumstances be justified ethically, what he says on this subject must not be taken in isolation from his teachings concerning peace. In fact, his articles on the *theology* of peace complete and perfect what he has written on the *ethics* of war. It must be added, too, that the principles of peace, because they are of the theological order and are based on revelation, greatly exceed his mere ethical principles in importance; just as all supernatural reality rises in measureless heights above the natural order.

Alas, that Christian men should neglect the bearings of the Gospel on this most serious problem of war, so often judging and acting (at best) according to principles that might equally be invoked by an upright pagan. Alas, that in so many discussions the highest standard appealed to is that of justice—vindictive justice at that—while the exigencies of grace and charity are allowed to go unexplored. To correct the one-sided view that comes from such an incomplete and inadequate understanding of Christian teaching, the following chapters will be devoted to examining the theology of peace, following the

(9) St. Ignatius of Antioch, *Letter to the Trallians.* See *The Apostolic Fathers*, Vol. I. (New York G. P. Putnam's Sons, 1930.) The preceding quotation is from the saint's *Letter to the Ephesians.*

guidance of the Angelic Doctor and the great Peace Encyclicals of the modern Popes.

2. The Possibility of Just War

1. Certain ideas, being more or less involved in all the issues to be discussed in the following pages, are accordingly prerequisite for the right understanding of the ideas that will be set forth in them. It is therefore necessary to describe these principles at the outset.

In emphasizing the supernatural character of peace, as also in advocating the application of supernatural principles and means to obtain it, there may seem to be an intent to deny the ethical principles concerning just war, or at any rate a tendency to slight them or view them with contempt or cast doubt on their validity. In truth, certain pacifists do take scandal at the fact that the Catholic Church admits, at least tacitly, the possibility of just warfare (10) and that this teaching has the

---

(10) Actually the Church has never formally defined this teaching. It has rather been worked out and established by her theologians and Doctors, and seems often to be simply taken for granted in her official documents. The closest thing to a definition is the condemnation by Pope Leo X of the following proposition: "*Proeliari adversus Turcos est repugnare Deo visitanti iniquitates nostras per illos.*" ("Since God visits our iniquities through the Turks, we offend Him by making war on them.")—Denziger-Bannwart, *Enchiridion Symbolorum*, No. 774.)

The error of the day held that since God used the Turks to punish the sins of Christians, it was wrong to make war on them. In condemning this error, the Church teaches that such war is *not against the Providential Dispensation by which God scourges the Christians through the Turks.* The Holy See does not here advocate war against the Turks nor assert that it is the best or only means of opposing them. *The use or propriety or justice of war is not the issue here:* the issue is whether there is a duty to oppose evil and the enemies of Christianity. The Church, while acknowledging the providential character of the sufferings inflicted by the Turks, nevertheless insisted that these enemies of Christianity were to be opposed. This is by no means a defense of war nor a doctrinal decision on its justice *as an instrument for settling international differences.* What the Church teaches here is that men are not to acquiesce in evil, that there is a duty to fight against it, that Christians are not to surrender their truth to the enemies of Christianity. As for war itself, the Holy See *does no more than take for granted the possibility of its justice*—a doctrine which it is also part of the purpose of this Introduction to vindicate.

The error condemned in this proposition is not unlike that of those who today hold that, since war is a scourge from God, it is useless and almost impious to attempt freeing mankind from this scourge. What these men forget is that God desires beatitude for men and not punishment: that He scourges them is due to their disobedience rather than to His redemptive will. While we should accept war as a scourge from God, it is nevertheless a religious *duty* to remove the guilt that brought down the punishment; and

direct authority of saints like Augustine and Thomas of Aquin. Such pacifists denounce all war as intrinsically evil and opposed to the spirit of Christ; and they think that, by so doing, they give honor to the Gospel, refusing to entertain the thought that its teaching can have anything in common with the monstrous iniquity of modern war. Consequently they are scandalized by those who reconcile a profession of Christianity with an acceptance of war. While the sincerity and ardor of these men is undeniable, it nevertheless remains true that they can take such a position only because they are unhampered by the knowledge of theology, the exigencies of reason, the need for intellectual consistency and doctrinal integrity. Such men, in the end, despite their good intentions, would throw Christianity into contempt and Evangelic pacifism into a hopeless muddle.

The affirmation of the possibility of a just war is a starting point for true Christian pacifism. This possibility is a thing not merely to be admitted by pacifists with more or less reluctance, but ought to be asserted and defended as a most important truth; otherwise their efforts for peace will be wanting a solid doctrinal foundation.

The reason for this is that, ultimately, a denial of the possibility of just war involves a denial of human rights. For if there are human rights, they should be respected, and they may be defended—in some cases they ought to be defended.

---

in performing this duty we work for the elimination of war. Similarly, while Christians should meekly accept the trials they suffer through God's enemies, as a punishment for their own sins, they must at the same time repent of these sins and fight against error and malice everywhere; they may not acquiesce in the evil of others any more than in their own.

Thus the condemnation of the above proposition does not mean that the Church advocates war as a means of settling international problems. The denunciations of war by modern Popes are too clear to allow any such conclusion as that! Indeed, it cannot even be said that the Church here advocates war as the best or only means, or an obligatory means, for overcoming even the Turks. In any case, as Father Stratmann observes, there is no parity between wars fought by Christian nations *among themselves* and those fought by Christian nations *against the external enemies of Christianity.* (*Peace and the Clergy*, p. 93. New York: Sheed and Ward, 1936.) As to the wars among the Christian nations of Europe, we know how the Holy See regards them when it describes them as "fratricidal": "Who would recognize them as brothers, whose Father is in heaven?" (Benedict XV, *Ad Beatissimi.*) Even in regard to the external enemies of Christianity, like the Turks, it seems clear that they might have been more successfully dealt with by the means proposed by St. Francis of Assisi than by force of arms.

Otherwise they are not really rights: evil men might violate them at their pleasure without incurring any guilt. If rights are not inviolable, to deny them or take them away would not be a real injustice. Who then could protest against war? If men have no real rights—to their lives, their homes, their families—how can there be an evil or horror in the destruction of property and life? Unless there were rights worthy of defense, wars would have no more moral significance than the internecine strife of the jungle, and tyranny or oppression should no more cause indignation than the slaughter of cattle for man's use as food. Such would be the inevitable conclusion were there no inviolable rights. That is why in our time rights are so cynically disregarded: the widespread moral relativism which looks upon human rights as a gift made by society to individuals or as the product of mere custom, without spiritual roots in human personality, has undermined the reality of rights and leaves them open to attack or "cancellation" by governments. Unless rights are real, with a spiritual reality, they cannot be inviolable; unless they are inviolable there is no wrong in appropriating or disregarding them. The denial of inviolable rights prepares the way for tyranny, oppression and war.

To oppose war it is necessary to experience the horror of war. We should be able to see the gravity and the extent of its injustice. We must be able to be genuinely indignant at its disregard of property, its razing of the great monuments of civilization, its destruction of the products of a people's industry and skill. We must be capable of holding in abomination the leveling of homes, not only by bombs and artillery fire, but also by conscription, deportation, enforced labor. We must be capable of being shocked to our depths by the wanton violation of God's holy temples, whether of stone or of flesh. Yet we simply cannot experience such horror and indignation unless we admit the existence of human rights, with all that they imply, realizing their inviolability and sacredness, together with the duty to affirm them, to respect them, to vindicate them—and to defend them. As without inviolable rights there can be no injustice, so without injustice there is no horror in war.

Whole peoples as well as individuals have rights, and their violation is a crime also. Hence the evil of aggressive war. Because these social rights are important, and the continuance of civilized society depends on respect for them, they are likewise to be defended; not to do so, as St. Augustine held, would be to hand the world over to wicked men. (11) Hence the doctrine concerning just war. Now when you further consider war as it actually is: with injured rights on both sides, but also with grievances on both sides, with mutual provocation and aggression, with international pledges and rights mutually disregarded, and, above all, with the rights to life and property of the common people everywhere abolished and swept away by governments bent on empire—then are you able to see and realize the immense iniquity of modern war. In the end, therefore, it is the violation of rights which ought to be preserved and defended that makes war so odious to civilized men, so abhorrent to Christian sensibilities.

Accordingly, St. Augustine and St. Thomas, by their doctrine of a just war, opened the way to our understanding and appreciation of the evils of war. They established and secured this first major position in a genuine Christian pacifism which should be rational as well as inspired. As we shall see, St. Thomas did much more than this, and on a higher plane of thought; but had he done only this, he would have done very much indeed. For this reason it is possible to compare his work for pacifism to the way in which he contributed to the definition of the Immaculate Conception.

As some wrongly take scandal at the Angelic Doctor's apparent justification of war, as though he were not of "the mind of Christ," others have similarly taken scandal at his apparent opposition to the doctrine of the Immaculate Conception, as though he were lacking in filial devotion to Our Lady. Yet if he opposed the Immaculate Conception, as defined in the nineteenth century, this was only because the meaning of this doctrine was not yet fully understood in his day. Nevertheless, that we are able to understand it today (in the limited sense in which it is possible to understand divine mysteries, as not being

(11) Quoted by St. Thomas, II II, 40, 1 ad 2.

in contradiction to reason), is largely due to this very opposition of St. Thomas. For it was he who stated the problem accurately, clearly indicated the requirements of reason, which the Immaculate Conception as understood at the time seemed to violate, and fixed the principles that were ultimately to clear the way for its definition. When the piety of some raced ahead of reason, St. Thomas exercised a restraining and guiding hand, basing himself on doctrine already defined and on the certainty that the truths of faith, although above reason, can never contradict it. If in the providence of God, it was not given to St. Thomas, but rather to his rival, Duns Scotus, to solve the difficulties, our indebtedness to Thomas is none the less real. His contribution to this great doctrine has been likened to that of a helm, which holds a ship in its right course, while the fervor of the Franciscan school, and of all other pious Christians, may be likened to the engines that drive the ship forward. "After God and His Church, it is to Scotus and his School that we are indebted for the definition of the Immaculate Conception, but it is to St. Thomas and his disciples that we are indebted for the definition of the true Immaculate Conception." (12)

Similarly, the principles of St. Thomas, by which he establishes the possibility of a just war, need not hinder us from seeking to eliminate war and inaugurate an era of true and lasting Christian peace. Once more, the holy Doctor's teaching will serve as a helm; it will keep our course true, give us doctrinal security as we go forward, preserve us from the shallows of sentimentality and the fatal rocks of unreason. St. Thomas could not foresee the problems of the twentieth century; he could not imagine the zeal with which modern men were to make the world uninhabitable. Nevertheless, he can assist us as we work for peace amid the debris left in the modern world by total war. Fidelity to his formal principles, (13) even at

(12) F. Marin-Sola. Quoted by Maritain, *St. Thomas Aquinas*, p. 137, footnote. (London: Sheed & Ward, 1933.) For a discussion of the difficulties involved in this definition, and the history of its development, see The Catholic Encyclopedia, article on "Immaculate Conception."

(13) This does not involve acceptance of all his applications. For example, he sanctioned the foundation of religious orders for military purposes. Yet in our day even the most fanatical believers in the myth that the two World Wars were crusades, did not go to the extreme of advocating the establishment of religious orders to carry them on.

the ethical level, and quite apart from his positive doctrine on peace which we shall shortly describe, is a prerequisite for a sound Christian pacifism.

2. It is now possible to understand, without scandal, the teaching that a just war is possible and does not conflict with the Gospel precept of love. Of course, to those who know *the reality* of war, it may seem faintly cynical to talk about killing an enemy out of love for him, as was done, for example, by the editor who, deploring the hate-propaganda of war time, recommended that bombardiers should loose their bombs with a prayer for the welfare of their victims. Yet no less than St. Thomas says that "it is licit to fight against enemies, that they may be restrained from sin; and this is for their good and the good of others." (14) Nor, granting the possibility of a just war, is there any other possible conclusion: if a war is just, it is in accord with the natural norms of morality; and the supernatural standards of the Gospel, although infinitely higher, cannot be in conflict with those of the natural order. Since both orders come from one God, the one self-consistent Truth, they must, in themselves, be in harmony with each other; so that supernatural charity can never be opposed to natural justice. If therefore it seems cynical to speak of killing enemies out of love, this must be attributed to the fact that *in reality* men themselves depart from the requirements of justice and carry on their wars out of motives other than love. The discrepancy is not to be attributed to any conflict in the two orders as they come from God, but rather in man's abuse of his powers and his failure to correspond with grace. Man, therefore, because of his freedom, can introduce disharmony between the two orders, and in fact he quite commonly does so. Nevertheless, in the ideal plan decreed by God, there can be no contradiction between the order of nature, which is ruled in accordance with justice, and that of grace, which is ruled by charity.

Another way to describe the harmony between the Gospel teaching on peace and the ethical principles of war is to say that Christianity is not opposed to war *as such*. To consider

---

(14) *Summa Theol.*, II II, 83, 8, ad 3. It is worthy of notice that St. Thomas does not here speak of *killing* enemies out of love. The difference is important as we shall show later. (Chap. IX.) See also footnote No. 16.

war *as such* is to strip it of the variable circumstances with which it is, of course, always clothed in every concrete instance; and the purpose of doing this is to study it in its essential character. It is to do something like the scientist does when he studies a lung, artificially constructed or preserved or kept alive, and quite apart from the relationship to the other organs and the actual conditions—say, bad air, poor nourishment, unhealthy working conditions—which affect the lungs in practice. The scientist follows such a procedure to study the nature and proper functions of the lung, which is best accomplished by isolating it and observing it under controlled "laboratory" conditions. So also to consider war *as such* is to strip it of the actual circumstances in which it is found and of the purposes for which in individual cases it is waged. It is then viewed, not in its concrete reality, but rather as an abstraction, as an idea constructed for purposes of isolated scientific study. Yet since, according to Catholic teaching, the circumstances of actions, especially their end, modify or altogether determine their morality in concrete cases, the assertion that Christianity is not opposed to war *as such* is a vastly different thing from saying that Christianity is not opposed to a concrete instance of war. While not opposed to war *as such*, Christianity may be and quite commonly is opposed to actual wars; for the circumstances of real war invariably bring it into opposition with the teachings of Christianity and even of natural morality.

In a parallel way it is said that gambling *as such* is not sinful —which is quite different from saying that gambling in all cases, or even in most cases, is without sin. Gambling *as such* is an abstraction and exists *in the mind*. In the concrete, gambling is invested with numerous circumstances, and here it is quite frequently sinful, made so by these very circumstances; as when by gambling a man deprives his family of necessities or exposes himself to danger through evil associations.

So also, war *as such* exists *only in the mind*: in concrete reality it is a quite different thing from what it is in the rarefied atmosphere of a philosopher's brain. Now when philosophers and theologians talk about war, they are invariably talking about war *as such*. When they say, like St. Thomas, that supernatural charity and the Sermon on the Mount are not opposed to war, they are here talking of war *as such*.

If it should then happen that a man in the street—faced by *a concrete instance of war* and forseeing the possibility that he may soon be a man in a barracks—questions these philosophers, or listens to their conversation or dips into their books, he of course hears that Christianity is not opposed to war *as such* and he decides to report on the matter to his fellows, for it is a discovery of great importance and will help him and his friends to settle an urgent practical problem. Accordingly he talks to these friends, or perhaps he writes articles or books, or makes public addresses. And others do the same; so that soon the news is circulated everywhere.

Unfortunately, however, these men have in all good faith made a subtle change in the "truth" they report. They heard the philosophers speak only about war *as such*. But they are not philosophers, and do not wholly understand the meaning of that phrase *as such* and therefore do not grasp its importance. They soon drop it, therefore (or mumble it uncomprehendingly), as a cumbersome and needless piece of technical jargon. And what they say then is simply that *Christianity is not opposed to war, meaning that Christianity is not opposed to a concrete instance of war,* for example the Second World War.

As a matter of fact, the man in the street (or in the barracks) is not looking at war *as such*; he sees something quite different from what the philosophers see. He sees war *as it is* in all its fearsome details. Yet he is sure that he has heard the philosophers aright and he has faith both in their knowledge and in their integrity. So he shrugs his shoulders, swallows his misgivings, develops a contempt for the drivel of pacifist sentimentality, and goes off to war—or at least exhorts others to go off

The ordinary man knows nothing of war *as such*. He merely is misled by the phrase. He is looking at the reality of war, at war as it actually is. The very circumstances of war, so concrete and real, from which the philosophers carefully abstract, are precisely what most impress and horrify him, make him wonder whether we are really civilized and how religion can approve such atrocities. What he sees is anything but a cold abstraction; it is an evil and frightening reality. He sees terrible engines of destruction, all the great resources of nations, as well as those of science and art, gathered, not to advance the interests of mankind, but to slaughter large sections of it; he sees the irreplaceable products and monuments of civilization wantonly destroyed; men conscripted for military service against their will, when all that they desire is the opportunity to live a quiet and peaceful life—whole peoples armed and uniformed for war; he sees the ruinous passions of hatred and revenge unloosed upon the world and creating dreadful havoc everywhere; he sees dead and wounded bodies—millions of men cruelly maimed or killed, unaware of the purpose of this slaughter and fully aware that past "crusades" have not made men happier or better; he sees the murder of women and children, of the sick and the aged—the complete demolition of entire cities, and he cannot but wonder whether this is any more justified by the alleged military necessity of his own side than it is by the cruelty of fanatical enemies; he sees famine, sometimes deliberately created, as by blockades—and more millions perishing; he sees a whole generation of young men corrupted by contempt of human life and the immorality that everywhere accompanies and follows war. Here is war as the ordinary man sees it: can you blame him if he is confused, perhaps cynical and hostile to religion, (15) when he hears bandied about that misleading truth, that half-truth, that inadequate and inaccurate statement of the truth, namely that Christianity is not opposed to war (*as such*)?

If you wish to see an example of war *as such*, something corresponding to the artificial lung that the doctor studies, do not go to the battlefields of the world where you find war *as*

(15) A sample of the doubts that arise in war time, even in the patriotic and those who accept the need for war, may be found in such articles as "Total War and Christianity," by Rev. J. C. Heenan, D.D. (*The Catholic Mind*, Jan., 1944.) "We have all heard the triumphant tones of radio announcers giving the number of homes destroyed in Hamburg. Some newspapers put the figure of civilian casualties no lower than 1,000,000. I do not believe such statements. But *suppose* they were true. Could we as Christians go on with Days of Prayer? Dare we ask God to bless our arms? Should we not be attempting to make Him an accomplice in evil deeds?" Whether or not the statistics are accurate, it is certain that the Allies did obliterate Hamburg (and other cities).

it is, the reality of war; where mere boys lose their limbs and their lives—yes, and their souls—in a hell of man's own devising. You will find a better approximation to war *as such* at Headquarters, where well-groomed officers plan strategy over sand tables and with pins on a map. This is about the nearest you will come to war as such; war without blood, without vile passion, without injustice, without evil. But do not go to the scarred islands of the Pacific, to the battlefields and ruined cities of Africa, Italy, Sicily, France, Germany, Russia, China, Japan. Here you will find a different kind of war, and the colorless and passionless abstractions of philosophers do not adequately depict its fearful outlines and lurid hues.

3. The upshot of all this is perfectly clear. Although the notion of just war is in complete harmony with the notion of charity, the concrete reality of war is never, or hardly ever, compatible with the practice of charity. In actual reality, wars are waged out of hatred, fanatical nationalism, the desire for revenge, greed, or the lust for power; and in their actual conduct they rely on unjust means, like lying propaganda, the murder of civilians, the bombing of cities. This means, in effect, that the possibility of just warfare is scarcely more than theoretical. The disinterested killing of enemies, or the attacking of them out of charity, as spoken of in the text cited a few pages back from St. Thomas, is quite different from the terrifying reality that is known in actual combat. (16) Men like St. Louis of France might serve to exemplify the perfect reconciliation of justice and charity; but, alas, there are not many such men: conformity to the example of St. Louis is as rare among soldiers as it is among kings. To kill out of charity, to wage war without violating the precepts of the Gospel—the thought of imperfect, carnal, or sinful men attempting to perform this feat brings to mind the duellists of a former age who, in a perfectly friendly and impersonal manner, killed and

(16) The practical difficulty is well illustrated by a question asked by a soldier's mother: "We pray for them to die in the state of grace; yet how can they die in the state of grace when they die with murder in their hearts?" St. Thomas himself distinguished the speculative and practical orders when, having shown the ideal harmony between just warfare and charity, he also said of soldiers that "They likewise sin if they are moved by private passion." Summa Theol., II II, 64, 7, 6.

carved up their dearest comrades with nice attention and careful fidelity to the detailed rules laid down for duelling by their brotherhood. There seems to have been something faulty about their notion of friendship. Dubious likewise at the very least is the charity of those who, ever requiring mercy for their own failings, are so exacting in their demands of justice from others.

Just wars, conducted politely in accord with the elaborate regulations of moralists, like a game of chess between friendly opponents, would be possible as an ordinary thing if men were living in *the state of pure nature* or of *integral nature,* that is, if they did not suffer from concupiscence and all their powers were intact, rightly ordered, and perfectly docile to reason. But man's nature is fallen, he is infected by concupiscence, his passions are strong, violent, rebellious, and as little prone to obey reason as his reason is to obey the impulses of grace. His wars, in practice, therefore, tend to depart markedly from the pattern of the chessboard and rather resemble the cruel struggle for survival that goes on among wild beasts—with this difference, that in the latter case a certain order is discernible, imposed, if not by reason, then at least by instinct.

To avoid possible misunderstanding, it is necessary before going on to insert an explanation of the above statement that just war is scarcely better than a theoretical possibility. This is not simply a restatement of the well-known teaching of certain contemporary theologians who propose a somewhat different view in almost identical terms, holding that just war in modern circumstances is only a theoretical or speculative possibility. These theologians derive their conclusion from a principle now quite firmly established as a notable modern contribution to the permanent ethics of war, viz., that a just war is possible at all only because in early stages of social development there does not exist a society of nations capable of dealing authoritatively with international problems. When such a society does exist, then just wars become only a theoretical possibility, ceasing to be a practical possibility for the same reason that private citizens may not take revenge on one another in a civilized community.

The difficulty with this principle, as with so many others, is in its application, which rests on a question of fact not easy to decide. If the principle itself is unassailable, the facts upon which the practical judgment must be made, to determine its application, are not wholly certain. It may be denied, for example, that international society has developed far enough in our day to be able to settle international disputes effectively and authoritatively; and if this is true, then just war is still a practical possibility. The theologians in question, however, are convinced that we have already attained to the possibility of a genuine international society—all that is lacking is good will; and they point to the achievements of the League of Nations—achievements which were very notable in many spheres of activity despite a tendency among some persons to speak of the League with contempt. If their contention is true, it would have to be concluded that even now just war is no more a practical possibility than the toleration of private revenge or private feuds among citizens.

While this principle is quite in line with the ideas defended here, and ought to be adopted as part of that body of doctrine which is the helm guiding us in our search for true Christian peace, (17) still, despite the similarity of phrasing, it is quite distinct from the conclusion that was stated above as coming from the considerations set forth in this Introduction. In saying that just war is scarcely more than a theoretical possibility, no reference is here made to the state of international society. Our conclusion is not based on an uncertain judgment concerning contingent events, but rather upon an unquestioned doctrine of the Faith; its basis is rather our knowledge of the feeble condition of fallen nature and the consequent difficulty of living up to the requirements of natural justice. Its meaning is that, due to the actual condition of human nature, the full and simultaneous realization of all the conditions required for a just war is a moral impossibility.

(17) No effort is made here however to decide the question of fact. This is perhaps incapable of final settlement at present. Certainly the *material* conditions and means required for an international society are abundantly present today; but in *actual fact* the international relations of modern governments, in war or peace, would do no honor to pirates or barbarians.

An examination of the effects of original sin will make this matter clearer. Although it is quite certain that fallen man, whether pagan or sinner, is able to perform some naturally good works without the special aid of divine grace, (18) it is equally certain, on the other hand, that fallen man, however great may be his natural powers or goodness, cannot observe the natural law in its entirety, or for any considerable length of time without the special assistance of divine grace. (19) It is this truth, quite apart from the state of international society at the present time, that makes the realization of a just war *morally impossible in practice.* By the rejection of Christ men not only become unable to attain to His sublime and supernatural way of life and ideal of society. Rejecting Him, they lose His grace, and having been left to work in this world with their natural powers impaired also, they are incapable of achieving perfectly even the ideal of a purely natural justice. Hence, although war may contain many individual acts of virtue—since even pagans and sinners may perform some good works—nevertheless it is impossible for men to keep all the acts and circumstances of war, over a long period of time and involving so many and such rigid requirements, up to that standard of natural justice which, apart from the Fall, would be within the scope of natural human powers.

In explaining this general doctrine, St. Thomas writes: "In the state of corrupt nature, man is deficient even in what he can do by nature; so that he cannot accomplish the total good (*bonum totum*) belonging to his nature by means of natural powers alone. On the other hand, because human nature is not wholly corrupted by sin or entirely deprived of its natural goodness, it can, even in its corrupt state, accomplish a certain limited amount of good (*aliquod bonum particulare*), like building houses, planting vineyards, and other works of this sort. However, it cannot achieve the entire good which is connatural to it, without any defect whatever." The saint then ends this passage with a fine illustration: "Thus also a sick man

(18) See Pohle-Preuss, *Grace: Actual and Habitual*, p. 55. (St. Louis: Herder Book Co., 1941.)

(19) *Ibid.*, p. 63.

is capable of some movement, but he cannot move perfectly, as a healthy man does, unless he is first healed with the help of medicine." (20)

In regard to keeping the precepts of the natural law, the Angelic Doctor says that in the state of original justice, when men's natural powers were unimpaired (hence also in the theoretical states of pure nature and integral nature), it would have been possible for him by means of these natural powers alone to fulfill the whole natural law. Not so, however, in the state of fallen nature: although in this condition men can observe some of the precepts of natural law, they cannot apart from grace observe them all. (21) Furthermore, in the state of original justice men could avoid both mortal and venial sin with only their natural powers. But in the state of fallen nature, they are able to avoid sin altogether only after the wounds consequent upon original sin have been healed by divine grace. Even then they will not be able to free themselves completely from venial sin due to concupiscence and sensuality.

And here the saint makes a further observation that is of the greatest practical importance in an age that has wholly rejected Christ: Unregenerate men, he says, while they will be able to avoid individual mortal sins, or to avoid all sin for a short time, will nevertheless not be able to persevere for long without sin. Moreover once they have fallen into grave sin, they are quickly carried on to others by that very fact; for, as St. Gregory says, "sin that is not soon removed by repentance, by its weight drags the soul into further sin." The reason for this is that the commission of mortal sin involves the choice of a creature as a final end, and such a choice determines subsequent actions also, as a traveler when he chooses his destination, thereby determines likewise the subsequent actions by which he will advance towards the desired goal. (22). "I find then a law that when I have a will to do good, evil is present with me. For I am delighted with the law of God, according

(20) *Summa theol.*, I II, 109, 2, c.
(21) *Ibid.*, Art. 3, c.
(22) *Ibid.*, Art. 8, c.

to the inward man: But I see another law in my members, fighting against the law of my mind, and captivating me in the law of sin, that is in my members." (23)

There is absolutely no reason to think that the case of war is exempt from this general doctrine. Indeed, if anything, it would be more difficult to achieve natural justice in war than at other times; to engage in killing as a profession and on a large scale, by its very nature, combined with the inherited weakness of fallen man, is more likely than any other pursuit or activity to break down restraint and cause human passions to rush forth in wild disorder, destroying by their violence whatever has been accomplished towards realizing the order of reason, virtue, and natural law.

It is not the purpose here to maintain that the idea of a just war was *never* realized in practice. That contention would require a historical inquiry, which, however useful it might be, does not fall within the scope of the present work; nor is such an inquiry necessary to vindicate our general conclusion. It is sufficient to say, as it clearly can be said, that a just war is very difficult to realize in practice—so difficult as to be morally impossible. This is a principle that is very well illustrated by history without depending on the contingent facts of history for its demonstration. It is a theological certainty. Moreover, although it is clear enough, even to a cursory glance, that there were few just wars in the past, the chief concern now is with the present. And it can be truthfully said, that whatever may have been the case with former wars, those of today are without moral justification: those wars, namely, which, proceeding from the evils and inner tension of Industrial Capitalism, have introduced universal conscription in violation of the common man's most intimate rights, have perverted science to purposes of destruction, have turned the whole world into a great battle ground, have trained entire nations to become killers and thus lose respect for human life, have brought wanton destruction and merciless slaughter everywhere. These are the wars which are fought today and to which the present principle is applied; and merely to recite

(23) Rom. 7, 21-23.

their motives, methods, and effects is to show how far they fall below, not merely the norms established by the Gospel, but also the laws written by the Creator in the very hearts of men.

If ever we might look to see the requirements for just warfare realized in practice, it would surely be in the conflicts of the Middle Ages, with their chivalry, their honest and forthright methods, their rigid code of honorable conduct, their quaint military customs and usages, which did indeed make them seem almost like a game of chess. Yet history reveals pitilessly the trivial and often gross purposes that were usually behind those fine and colorful military displays—purposes which secretly killed, at the start, any possible righteousness in the wars they inspired, that is to say, killed it in their motives, which are the center and heart of human actions; just as some deadly virus might attack a seed and so destroy a plant before it begins to grow. Even the Crusades are not beyond question: St. Bernard, after preaching a Crusade, attributed its disaster to the gross misconduct of the Crusaders. (24) Human nature was also strong in the Ages of Faith; concupiscence and the corruption left by the Fall remain even in Christians. When it is said that the natural law can be kept with the assistance of grace, this means, not only that grace must be given by God, but also that men on their part must accept it and correspond with it. However powerful in itself, grace is powerless to sanctify men without their cooperation. Accordingly, we are forced to the paradoxical conclusion that only those who live supernatural lives can perfectly preserve the natural virtues and the natural law. Mediocre Christians, because of their neglect of grace, are scarcely better able than the unregenerate to realize in practice the ideal of reason and the good that is connatural to human powers. It is more difficult than most patriots dream to fulfill all the requirements of just warfare.

Now if the concrete realization of a just war was very difficult in the Ages of Faith, when men had sacramental assistance and at least some perception of the absolute need of supernatural life, what shall we say of this age which has so completely repudiated the teaching of Christ and neglected the

---

(24) Luddy *op cit.*, p. 596 *et seq.*

means of grace that He has left to us? The modern world has become wholly secularized. The Church of Christ has been reduced to the position of one sect among many, a minority group; and, besides, many of its own members have been deeply infected by the spirit of the age. Naturalism dominates the conduct of the men of today; that is to say, the code which now largely governs human action is a corrupt paganism that gives free rein to the disorderly tendencies of fallen nature. What can be thought of the ability of such an age to achieve the ideal of natural justice? St. Thomas has already answered that question for us: While able to perform isolated acts of virtue, unregenerate man cannot wholly avoid sin nor keep free from it for any long time. And when he once begins to sin, there is no stopping: sin leads to sin, then to the habit of sin; and men are left to drag out their lives in weariness and despair at the level of beasts while moral impotence prevents them from reaching, and finally from seeing, the light and truth of God. Such, at any rate, is what would be expected on the basis of Catholic doctrine concerning the need of grace and the weakness of fallen nature. And the concrete reality of war matches perfectly these expectations. Here, for example, is how the highest authority in Christendom measures the reality of war against the norms of the Gospel and of natural morality: "A year has gone [since his last anniversary address to the Cardinals], a brief span of time, and yet so filled with hate and mournful happenings and unmeasured, unspeakable suffering; the terrible tragedy of the World War, as it unfolds itself before and around us, has reached a pitch and kind of frightfulness which *smite and shock every Christian and human* sense." (25) Such words give unmistakable evidence to the conclusion that, although Christianity is not opposed to war *as such,* it is opposed to wars in actual reality. Therefore, we must in practice oppose every concrete instance of war.

(25) Pope Pius XII, Address to College of Cardinals on his feast day, June 2, 1944.

70
x7
CATICH

I

TRUE PEACE AND FALSE PEACE

1. It is first of all necessary to know in what sense Christ came to bring peace; then we can go on to inquire how Christianity can procure it. For if Christ, as the Scriptures tell us, came into the world accompanied by a divine promise of peace for men, nevertheless there is a kind of peace which He will not give—which He came, in fact, to destroy. If He said, "Peace be to you," (1) He had before spoken far different words: "Do not think that I came to send peace upon earth; I came not to send peace, but the sword." (2)

How shall we reconcile these two apparently contradictory statements? St. Thomas does so (3) by distinguishing between *true* and *false* or *apparent* peace. He explains that peace consists in a certain quieting and satisfaction of the desires of the soul; and since these desires may be satisfied either by their true good, as intended by the Creator, or by some false or apparent good which cannot bring true satisfaction, so true peace arises from the quieting of all desire in *our true last end*, while false peace is the fair-seeming, but delusive, and insecure tranquillity that comes of making an end of material goods. The first mistake made by the irreligious (or unreligious) seeker for peace is to base his hopes on material wealth and power; the first truth that the Church points out is that an entirely different basis of peace must be found. "Now the whole secret of this divine philosophy is that what are called the goods of this mortal life have indeed the appearance of good, but not the reality; and, therefore, it is not in the enjoyment of them that men can be happy. In the divine plan, so far are riches and glory and pleasure from bringing happiness to man, that if he really wishes to be happy, he must rather for God's sake renounce them all. . . . In no other way can individuals and nations attain to peace." (4)

---

(1) St. Jo. 20, 21.
(2) St. Matt. 10, 34.
(3) *Summa Theol.*, II II, 29, 2 ad 2.
(4) Pope Benedict XV, *Ad Beatissimi*.

True peace is a tranquillity enjoyed by the soul because all its desires and aspirations have been fulfilled according to right order and by their real good. This is why St. Augustine defines peace as *the tranquillity of order.* False peace, on the other hand, since it arises from the enjoyment of earthly pleasures, is as fleeting, uncertain, and unsatisfying as are these pleasures. Moreover, it is sure to come to a violent end because of the disorder that unmortified sensual desires introduce into the soul, causing turmoil there and inciting those so aroused to resist—or to attack, should there be need—all who would stand in the way of their selfish gratification. True peace is a reality, solid, clearly visible in the penetrating light of faith; when possessed, it satisfies the deepest needs of human nature. False peace is a mirage; it is formed of no more substantial stuff than the vapors which arise from disorderly passions and desires. While squandering the energies of those who seek it, it disappears at the very instant at which they try to possess it. Instead of satisfying, it makes its possessors ever more restless and dissatisfied; and it brings them into inevitable conflict with others who, in their avid search for this kind of "peace," reach for the same glittering baubles.

It is to be feared that, for the most part, when men speak of peace as a desirable end, as also when they formulate peace policies and sit down at peace conferences, the kind of peace which they have in mind is the false peace which Jesus came to destroy. Men love what they call peace because war means that they must give up a life of enjoyment to accept hardship, discipline, and sacrifice. War disturbs the outer tranquillity of events, tears them away from accustomed comforts, forces them to relinquish their ordinary employments and the pursuit of wealth, exposes them to danger and pain and even death. Naturally, therefore, they seek for peace. But clearly, in such a case, their motives are low and selfish. There is no high purpose, no idealism, directing their search, no spiritual motive animating their efforts. What they want is, not really peace, but the opportunity of sensual enjoyment free from the danger of disturbance; like that of a house-dog dozing beside the kitchen stove. Even those who are deeply afflicted by the cruel separation from loved ones which war involves are too often earthly, sensual, selfish in their desire for peace. It is not "the peace of God" that they want *for all men*; they are thinking too much of themselves and their own happiness; and even their notion of happiness is likely to be earthly and gross.

Even when men *pray* for peace, it is not always for the peace of God, but too frequently for the false, worldly peace. Hence God is as little prone to answer their prayers as He is to bless their efforts to obtain it. "You ask and receive not, because you ask amiss; that you may consume it on your concupiscences." (5)

It could scarcely be otherwise, men remaining as they are. The carnal mind cannot understand the things of God, which are spiritual; (6) it cannot but misconceive, materialize, and degrade Christ's promise of peace. Because, too, so many Christians have not themselves "the mind of Christ," but rather are "conformed to this world," their conception of peace is similar to that of "them who are without." Accordingly, the means by which they propose to obtain peace are the same as those on which the world relies, being the only means of which the carnal mind can conceive—i.e., diplomacy, alliances, pacts, treaties, threats, force, war. You may examine history for the record of success in the efforts that have depended on such means. Their past, you must admit, does not hold forth much hope for their future.

Such is the peace of the world, of which our Lord says, "Not as the world giveth, do I give unto you." (7) At the worst, this peace is "earthly, sensual, devilish," (8) being sought in disregard of God and in contempt of His law. At the best it is but a human and natural good; so that men think to obtain it by human and natural means. That the most earnest and enlightened efforts to obtain even this human good have failed is due, in the first place, to the secret treachery which is in human nature itself as a consequence of the Fall—a treachery that through our darkened understanding first of all misrepre-

(5) St. James, 4, 3.
(6) I Cor. 2, 14.
(7) St. John, 14, 27.
(8) St. James, 3, 15.

sents peace in the manner described, then encourages that indulgence in sensual desire which brings the short-lived and delusive peace that is false, while rendering impossible any realization of the true "peace of God." This treachery of fallen nature is what sets at naught the most careful calculations and the most determined efforts of a merely human pacifism. There is also, secondly, the fact that God, who is omnipotent, has Himself promised to destroy the peace which the world esteems: *not peace, but the sword.* The One whom men look to for aid in securing their false "peace" is the very One who is defeating their every effort. Despairing of their prayers, they then cry out, *"We looked for peace and no good came: for a time of healing and behold fear."* Yet they never learn and never change because they follow false prophets who cry out eternally their lying promise, *"Peace, peace, when there is no peace."* (9)

2. If the world is to become truly serious in its desire for peace, it must be "reformed in the newness of its mind." (10) It must have "the mind of Christ"; so that, purged of its preoccupation with false and worldly peace, it may be ready to study, then to pursue, "the peace of Christ." Otherwise it will go on dignifying with the name of peace those brief and uncertain periods of armistice in which nations, exhausted by war but unrepentant, prepare themselves bravely for new slaughters.

Cleansed in mind, therefore, by purity of life and meditation on the Gospels, men will be able to understand that, just as false peace arises from love of the fleeting goods of earth, true peace comes from the love of spiritual things. "Of this Peace of Christ. . . . We can repeat what the Apostle has said of the Kingdom of God which also rules by love—The Kingdom of Christ *is not meat and drink.* (11) In other words, the Peace of Christ is not nourished on the things of earth, but on those of heaven." (12)

They will be able to see then only how this peace is to be

---

(9) Jer. 8, 5; 8, 11.
(10) Rom. 12, 2.
(11) Rom. 14, 17.
(12) *Ubi Arcano Dei.*

procured: that it can be only by establishing the reign of Christ. "It is, therefore, a fact which cannot be questioned that the Peace of Christ can only exist in the Kingdom of Christ—'the Peace of Christ in the Kingdom of Christ.' It is no less unquestionable that, in doing all we can to bring about the re-establishment of Christ's Kingdom, we will be working most effectively toward a lasting world peace." (13) The Kingdom of Christ must be established on earth.

If you say that this is impossible, then you mean that Christianity is impractical and you condemn mankind to an unending succession of murderous—rather, fratricidal—wars, each one more horrible than the one before. The goal of true peace, however, is not impossible, for Christianity is not impractical. More will be said on this point in another place; let us merely remark now in passing that the motto selected by Pope Pius XI (surely a "representative" Catholic!) to describe the purpose of his pontificate was precisely this, "The Peace of Christ in the Kingdom of Christ."

If only we would put the same zeal that is spent in pursuing the vain pleasures of the world into seeking after the things of God, men would soon see that it is not necessary to have guns and armies, and all the monstrous evils that come in the wake of war, in order to have a short, uncertain, delusive travesty of peace!

3. If you should object, in surprise, that such a proposal is not new, that, in fact, the Church has been exerting herself in missionary effort during all the centuries of her existence, with the purpose of establishing the Kingdom of Christ on earth, then it must be admitted that it would be foolish to deny so patent a fact and there is no intention of doing so here. But these official efforts, as the past testifies, are not enough. If, as we are told, a nation organized for *total* war can only be opposed by another nation similarly organized, it is no less certain that the total war effort must be met by a total peace effort. *All* our resources must be placed at the disposal of the Prince of Peace. Besides giving financial support to missionary enterprises, we must ourselves work to convert

(13) *ibid.*

the heathen, satisfying for their sins by our own sacrifices and winning by our prayers the graces which they need to pass "from darkness to light."

However, the extension of Christ's Church is not simply a matter of converting heathens. There is the still more difficult task of converting Christians. (14) These must begin, not merely to profess their faith, but to live it. While praying and sacrificing for others, they must meanwhile strive to sanctify their own lives, that their prayers and works may be acceptable to the All-Holy God. If they do this, they will soon learn, as St. Teresa remarks, that no one ever becomes holy *alone.* If they do not, then their lives, according to the laws which regulate the distribution of graces in the divine economy, will continue to nullify in advance the work of Christian missionaries.

When certain French Bishops of North Africa once sent an invitation to Arab notables to attend a religious conference, the latter sent back an insulting and historic reply: "Why do you wish us to become Christians? Is it to become like those we see here? Thanks, but it is better that we remain Mohammedans!" (15) In this meaningful and (unfortunately) typical incident is revealed what holds up the establishment of the kingdom of Christ, what alone makes the realization of the full Christian ideal "impractical." It is the infidelity, the negligence, the disobedience of Christians; it is their want of genuine love for Jesus Christ. Conversion, like charity, must begin at home. We, of course, like to think of ourselves as Christians already; yet in fact this is an age in which "men have fallen away miserably from Jesus Christ" and in which "the habit of life which can be called really Christian has in great measure disappeared." (16)

To follow Jesus—not merely as "nominal" or "practical"

---

(14) "As in all the stormy periods of this history of the Church, the fundamental remedy today lies in a sincere renewal of private and public life according to the principles of the Gospel *by all those who belong to the fold of Christ*, that they may be in truth the salt of the earth to preserve human society from total corruption."—Pius XI, *"Divini Redemptoris."*

(15) National Magazine for the Society for the Propagation of the Faith, January-February, 1943.

(16) Pope Pius XI, *Ubi Arcano Dei.*

Catholics whose religion ends with regular Church attendance and a routine reception of the sacraments, if it goes so far, but to obey His laws, to imitate His example, to accept His valuation of human life and the world, to oppose the world and renounce its pleasures, to deny one's self, to go with Him to Calvary, to drink of His chalice—that is what is to be done if Christians would work for and realize, and not merely discuss and study, the peace of Christ. Since this has not been done, men remaining satisfied apparently with gazing, from afar or merely in imagination, at the abstract qualities of Christian peace, it is not hard to understand why even sincere desires and prayers for peace have gone unanswered. If your house is on fire and you rush to a neighbor for aid, and the neighbor, in charity, comes to help you, doing everything that he can, while you meanwhile do nothing at all to save your own house—what will the neighbor do when he at length discovers your idleness and indifference? Surely he will let your house burn, seeing that, since it is not of sufficient value to cause you to exert yourself, there is scarcely reason why he should jeopardize his life in an attempt to save something that you really do not want. When you call upon the assistance of others, it is no more than reasonable to expect that you do all that is possible to help yourself.

So also God, when He hears our appeals for peace, requires that we on our side do what we can—that we, in a word, observe the laws and fulfill the conditions that are necessary for disposing ourselves for this divine gift. ". . . No real peace, most certainly not the longed-for peace of Christ, can exist unless the teaching, the commandments, *the example of Christ are faithfully followed in public and private life . . .*" (17) If we fail to do what is in our power, then God *cannot* hear our plea, anxious as He is to give us this most beautiful of His gifts. God does not force His graces upon us. His eternal plan requires that we cooperate with Him in order to obtain our salvation and all the other privileges that come in its train.

---

(17) Pope Pius XI, *ibid.*

II

THE CHARACTER OF PEACE

1. Warned against error by the knowledge of what is meant by false peace, we are prepared to understand better the nature and properties of true peace.

If, as we have observed, true peace is spiritual, it must also be *interior.* "Let the peace of Christ rejoice *in your hearts.*" (1) It is not therefore to be attained mechanically, or by external means—by treaties, political alliances, economic agreements. These should be the expression of interior peace; and, if they are not, then they are of no more value than the paper on which they are written, as modern history clearly demonstrates. Peace must be in the hearts of men, otherwise the most skillful diplomacy or the most far-seeing policies cannot be successful. During the "peace" that obtained after World War I, Pope Pius XI was constrained to write: "Peace indeed was signed in solemn conclave between the belligerents of the late war. This peace, however, *was only written into treaties. It was not written into the hearts of men,* who still cherish the desire to fight one another and to continue to menace in a most serious manner the quiet and stability of civil society." (2) We are witnesses of the results.

St. Thomas throws light on this matter by distinguishing between *peace* and *concord.* (3) Peace, he observes, includes concord; so that there will be concord among men wherever there is true peace. Not *vice versa,* however: for there may be concord among various persons or groups, because of an agreement in seeking together certain desirable ends, without there being true and lasting peace. How is this? Because peace includes, beyond a mere external or limited agreement, the satisfaction and tranquillizing of all the interior desires and appetites of those who possess it.

---

(1) Col. 3, 15.
(2) op. cit.
(3) *Summa Theol.*, II II, 29, 1.

No one, whatever his material advantages, has a truly peaceful heart as long as he does not have all that he desires. "Man's heart is not at peace as long as he does not have whatever he wishes for; this is true even when he has some of the goods that he wants but cannot possess other desirable things which he is lacking." (4) The false peace that we obtain from the possession of material things is not stable or lasting because of the things we do not possess. True peace requires that the appetites be wholly stilled.

It is evident that such peace is not to be bought cheaply. The peaceful man is in repose; he has ended his search; he has found an unfailing spring of genuine happiness; there are left in him no unsatisfied desires that can bring disquiet to his soul.

The unpeaceful man, on the contrary, is restless, discontented, ever in search of new satisfactions. This at once brings him into conflict with his neighbors. Seeking happiness in material goods, where true joy is not to be found, his desires are left unsatisfied and the meager pleasures that he finds only serve to whet his appetite. His neighbors are not safe from his envy and greed. Peace is then broken because men with covetous hearts come into conflict over the material goods in which, seeking happiness, they find, besides their own disquiet, occasion for contention, hatred, strife, and every evil passion. There can be no peace among men unless there is peace within them.

Worldly-minded men, united for the pursuit of some limited good, will be in concord to the extent of their agreement, but their "peace" is unstable because of their unsatisfied, conflicting desires which the agreement does not cover. These desires, roving about like bandits, will sooner or later clash with the passions of others in search of the same plunder. Thus there may be a certain limited, temporary, precarious concord even among murderers or pirates, like the treaties that are signed by modern nations. Such agreements, however, no matter how finely phrased, cannot bring peace because there is not peace in the souls of the peoples who make them. You cannot get water from a dry spring.

---

(4) St. Thomas, *ibid.*

On the other hand, interior peace satisfies the heart, the desires, the passions; it therefore removes the cause of conflicts and the occasion of war. Discord comes when opposed passions seek satisfaction in defiance of one another, as when avaricious men (or nations) come into conflict over the source of wealth. St. James says that wars are caused by "your concupiscences, which war in your members." (5) If, however, the appetite for happiness is satisfied, if passions and desires are kept under the control and guidance of reason and faith, there is no cause or occasion for envy and greed, conflict and war. A man with peace in his heart easily lives in peace with his fellows.

Those who work for peace without laboring to obtain for themselves and their fellows that which satisfies the heart will be disappointed and disillusioned. Not without weighty doctrinal reasons did Pope Pius XI lay it down that the very first step towards establishing world peace is to labor towards bringing peace to human hearts: "First and most important of all for mankind is the need of spiritual peace. We do not need a peace that will consist merely in acts of external or formal courtesy, but a peace which will penetrate the souls of men. . . ." (6)

The first really practical move towards world peace—though "practical men" will scoff at the idea—is, not to call an international conference of statesmen and somehow compel them to accept the formal terms and principles of a Christian peace, but rather to provide for the deepest aspirations of the soul, to satisfy its secret desires, to still its restlessness. If this is done, then a marvelous thing will happen. You have seen how, when a pebble is thrown into a pond, tiny ripples start out in all directions from the point where it enters the water, then move outward in concentric, circular waves that widen and increase as they go. When many pebbles are thrown at once, the circles intersect and merge at a thousand points, and the whole surface of the water is broken by innumerable minute waves spreading in every direction. So does the peace of the heart spread and embrace all the works of men. When

(5) St. James, 4, 1.
(6) *Ubi Arcano Dei.*

many enjoy it, each becomes a center from which it bursts forth and flows outward in every direction, touching human activity at innumerable points and bringing harmony and tranquillity to all the relationships of life and society.

But first means first; and when the Vicar of Christ says that the first and most important step is to bring peace to the hearts, then this is exactly what ought to be done; and it ought to be done first. As it happens, however, men persistently, and on principle (Catholics as well as others), refuse to take this first and most important step; and, as long as this is so, it is simply folly to expect that any other measures, however earnestly considered or wisely planned, can possibly avail. Hence the failure of peace movements, whether secular or religious. They do not fail because peace is intrinsically impossible, but because men do not use the necessary and proportionate means for obtaining peace. Even religious peace efforts do not *in practice* give first place to revealed truth by placing chief reliance on spiritual means and measures. They rely on diplomacy and are concerned only with political plans, economic agreements, international conferences, etc., etc., etc.

2. These considerations enable us to set down another characteristic of true peace. Besides being interior and spiritual, it is also *supernatural*, a free gift of God, belonging to the divine and not to the merely human order.

Hence the Scriptures call it the "peace *of God*" (7) and "the peace *of Christ*." (8) Jesus Himself carefully distinguishes His peace from that of the world. "Peace I leave with you, *my* peace I give unto you: not as the world giveth, do I give unto you." (9)

St. Paul places peace among the twelve fruits of the Holy Spirit, (10) showing that it is produced in the heart by the activity of God and is therefore no mere natural sentiment nor the product of natural affection, however noble. It exceeds the human and natural order altogether and therefore cannot be produced by human or natural means. Only the Spirit of God

(7) Phil. 4, 17.
(8) Col. 3, 15.
(9) St. John, 14, 27.
(10) Gal. 5, 22.

and divine grace can create it in hearts that are properly disposed. This does not mean that men can themselves do nothing to bring about peace. But it does mean that their efforts must be carried forward on the supernatural plane and are to consist in using whatever measures are available for inducing the Spirit of God to enter human hearts. So far as man can do anything about it, peace is the fruit of supernatural living; and no natural means whatever, no matter how excellent or wise or powerful, can avail to produce an effect that simply exceeds all the powers of the whole natural order. The Christian peace effort cannot rely on intellectual or political means, but must rather consist in a whole-hearted response to the Apostle's, "I admonish thee that thou stir up the grace of God which is in thee." (11)

Although it is true that the Holy Fathers, in various pronouncements, have insisted upon some kind of international society of nations as a requisite for peace, nevertheless the formation of such a league (or whatever it might be called) does not belong to the soul or essence of their plan but is rather its effect or concrete expression in the political order. Those who, occupied exclusively with the political aspects of the Holy See's recommendations, think by such means to achieve true Christian peace, at once misunderstand and misinterpret both Papal and Catholic teaching.

The Peace Movement is primarily a religious movement. Specifically, it is Christian. Not only is it true that a Christian can be a pacifist; it is also true that no one except a Christian can be a pacifist. By a Christian, of course, is meant a Catholic; for only in the Catholic Church is to be found the fullness of Christianity.

St. Thomas relates peace to supernatural charity, teaching that it is an act of this virtue. In our day Pope Pius XI has made this doctrine his own: "The Angelic Doctor expresses it most aptly, as is his wont, saying that peace, true peace, is a thing rather of charity. . . . Peace itself is really and specifically an act of charity." (12) Let it be kept in mind that charity

---

(11) II Tim. 1, 6.
(12) *Op. Cit.*

is no mere activity of the will; it is not a sentiment that proceeds from the human heart. It is divine grace operating in the soul. It is not to be brought into the soul by refining the affections or educating the sentiment; belonging to the supernatural order, it can be infused into the soul only by God.

Here is revealed a basic misconception that nullifies most peace efforts before they have begun. Outside the Church even the most idealistic peace work scarcely aims higher than justice. Among Catholics, too, is heard much about justice, little about the supernatural order, the order of charity. Yet justice cannot bring peace directly; however important and necessary is this natural virtue, it could never produce a good that belongs to an altogether different and higher order; any more than an animal brain, however perfect, could write a poem or a symphony.

At best, St. Thomas teaches, justice can aid in bringing about peace only indirectly, that is, by removing obstacles which stand in its way—such obstacles, for example, as the exploitation of one nation by another, or some violation of right. Accordingly, though all nations and peoples might be conceivably brought together in an order of justice, this would still not be able to create a true Christian peace. The forces of the supernatural order alone can bring this into existence. Only by bringing their lives and their society to conform with the great laws that govern the supernatural economy can men live at peace with themselves and with one another.

There is no other way. You may call as many meetings as you like. You may write as many books as you like. You may by diplomacy secure the interest and good will of as many statesmen as you like. You may draw up proposals for just international arrangements; and let us suppose that you can persuade governments to adopt them. All this will be quite useless if you neglect first to set about bringing into souls, through purely supernatural means, new increases of grace and charity.

3. How disheartening is it to observe, day after day, how writers and speakers, religious and secular, call on *the nations of the world,* or their leaders, to do this or that, to adopt this

program or to subscribe to that principle. It is for the See of St. Peter—and, within a more limited sphere, for Bishops—to lay down terms and conditions of peace even for the princes of the world. But for the rest of us, how idle to address pretentious counsels to the great of this world, who will pay no attention to us, or even know that we have spoken, while at the same time we neglect the work that is close at hand, the work that is first and most important, the work that is particularly ours as Christians and which even the humblest can engage in at once: the work of converting hearts, beginning with our own! When you hear of a group of men, or of a peace organization, taking up in earnest the insistent demand of the Holy Fathers for spiritual renewal, and outlining a program of spiritual and supernatural activity designed to carry men forward to holiness—a program to the acceptance of which it pledges first of all its own members, and not the heads of states —then you will know that peace, true peace, the peace of Christ, has begun its long delayed conquest of this troubled world.

Vain, likewise, is the hope of those who think to obtain peace by armies and the use of force. Surely their confidence cannot be said to have a basis in Catholic doctrine—

> "Some put their hope in chariots, others in steeds,
> But we in the name of the Lord Our God.
> They are entangled and fall;
> But we arise and hold ourselves erect. . . ." (13)

"To hope," writes Pope Pius XII, "for a decisive change exclusively from the shock of war and its final issue is idle, as experience shows. . . . No, Venerable Brethren, safety does not come to peoples from external means, from the sword, which can impose conditions of peace but does not create peace. Forces that are to renew the face of the earth should proceed from within, from the spirit." (14)

Truth compels us to go even further in drawing out these corollaries. There is an insistent demand from many Catholic

(13) Ps. 19. 8-9.
(14) Pope Pius XII, *Summi Pontificatus.*

quarters that the Holy Father be included in the conferences that frame the conditions of peace; and that he has been ignored in the past is held responsible for the fact that we do not have a Christian peace in the world. But how futile is the hope to have a Christian peace simply by securing the Pope's presence at the peace conferences! Were we to succeed, by agitation, in having him invited to these conferences—and even to have him preside—our triumph would be only apparent and in fact delusive, unless there were in the souls of men that charity which alone can give a foundation of reality to Christian peace. Even a Christian peace is no good if it is written on paper only and not in the hearts of Christians, or if it is agreed to by men who do not actually represent the souls and sentiments of the peoples for whom they claim to speak. Pope Pius XI declared as much when he said: "When, therefore, States and peoples shall hold it as their sacred solemn duty, in home and foreign affairs, to obey the teachings and precepts of Jesus Christ, then at length they will enjoy good peace among themselves, there will be mutual trust, and they will be able to settle peacefully any controversies that may arise." (15)

We are wasting our time, as well as proving faithless to our essential duty as Christians, when we demand a place for Catholic representatives and Christian principles at peace conferences while in the meantime neglecting to dispose our spiritual resources for creating the conditions which are necessary to establish genuine, interior, supernatural peace. If we leave the generals to win the peace, it is to be expected that they will demand to fix its conditions. It is we Christians who should win the peace; and it is we alone who can *bring true peace.* And then, having accepted our responsibility, may we fittingly demand a place for our representatives at the conference. No doubt the Pope, simply as Christ's Vicar, and independently of the suffrages of his children, has the right to state the terms of a just and Christian peace. It is nevertheless up to us, his children, to establish within our souls those spiritual conditions which alone can make the Holy Father's affirmations and rul-

(15) *Ubi Arcano Dei.*

ings a reality and not merely the description of a remote ideal. He does not depend on our suffrage; and yet the quality of *our* lives, and not *his* pen or *his* presence at world parleys, can alone give solidity and truth to the establishment of Christian peace.

III

THE WAY TO INTERIOR PEACE

1. If peace is a Gift of the Spirit, how is it to be brought into human life and society? Are we to sit and wait for it? If we do, we are likely to be kept waiting! To affirm the supernatural character of peace is not to release men from effort; it is, on the contrary, to summon them to the highest possible spiritual effort. In order to be practical, however, we must be definite; we must know and set down beforehand the nature of this effort and the direction it is to take; as men, before undertaking a journey, decide their destination and manner of travel.

In outlining a practical procedure, it is necessary to keep in mind the two kinds of peace. First of all, we have said, peace is the union of all the appetites within the soul in the possession of their true good, the repose of the heart in that which completely satisfies desire. Secondly, it is the union of the wills and desires of a number of individuals (or groups) who seek together something which they recognize as good. The former, interior peace, dwells in the heart; the latter is political, or social, peace.

The two kinds belong together; you cannot have one without the other. As interior peace overflows into that which is external and social, so the latter is simply the visible manifestation of that which is interior. It is not merely that interior peace precedes political peace and establishes conditions without which the latter cannot be realized, as we have already observed. The relationship is still closer than this. Only when those who live together are united in *all the great ends* of human life, or at any rate *in the final end* that dominates the whole of life, will they be able to have true peace among themselves, strongly rooted, stable, complete. Anything less is what we have called concord; and concord is not peace. If a number of men are running towards the same goal, they move together, in concert, and do not interfere with one another; but if they are striving for different or opposite goals—as in a crowded street or a football game—there will certainly be clashing and contention. Peace requires a union of wills, a union of effort, a union of purpose.

Thus all parties of a genuine political or social peace must be united to their true last end. Only the true last end of life can satisfy the desires within the heart of every individual; so that only by devoting himself to the attainment of this end can each man possess interior peace. Furthermore, nothing except the *true* last end of life can be acceptable to *all* men. Nothing else provides a common ground upon which *all* can *fully* agree; nothing else, therefore, can be a basis for true and lasting peace. Therefore the wills of the many can be brought together in the pursuit of their supreme good (the union which is the very essence of social peace), only if the individuals who compose the many are united within themselves, that is when their appetites and passions are purified, rectified, and brought into harmony under wills that regulate all things in accordance with the highest requirements of truth. This is why social peace is but the external form and expression of interior peace and proceeds from the latter as from its source. Grumblers and malcontents can as easily be formed into a happy family as unpeaceable men into a peaceable society.

The first step towards social peace is unanimity in choosing the true last end of life. The second step is to outline a program for the use and disposition of whatever means lead to that end.

2. First let us speak of peace in the individual. What is the true last end of human life? No need for a Christian to ask that question! "Our hearts were made for Thee, O God, and they will never rest until they rest in Thee." (1) And again, "As the hart panteth after the fountains of running water, so my soul panteth after Thee, my God." (2) The soul can satisfy itself fully only in God. "We know that every creature groaneth and travaileth in pain, even until now," (3) that is,

(1) St. Augustine, *Confessions*, Chap. 1.
(2) Ps. 41, 2.
(3) Rom. 8, 22.

until the coming of Christ. Each soul groans and travails until the manifestation of Christ within it; that is, until it learns to know God by love.

This being so, the author of the Imitation would have us seek peace also in God: "Grant me also, above all things that can be desired, that I may rest in Thee, *and fully in Thee pacify my heart.* For Thou, O Lord, art *the very true peace of heart* and perfect rest of body and soul, and without Thee all things be grievous and unquiet. Wherefore in that peace which is in Thee, one high, one blessed, one endless goodness, shall I always rest me." (4)

Why is this? Because charity, or love for God, unites man to his true last end, and at the same time, and for this very reason, it is the cause and source of peace. "God is love; and he that abideth in love abideth in God and God in him." (5) Love joins the soul to God. Therefore, it is also love, love for God, as St. Thomas teaches, (6) that creates interior peace in the heart. The precept of charity, in demanding that we love God with our whole hearts, our whole minds, and all our strength, unites us to our true last end, even obliges us to seek it, and thereby causes peace to enter the soul.

You may see here why peace is an effect of love; you may also see why, as an effect of love, it can be achieved only by obedience to the commandment of love. Charity—complete charity, as prescribed by the commandment—concentrates all the faculties of our nature upon one supreme object; it exhausts the energies of the soul in one all-absorbing quest; it brings together in one tremendous effort of love all the soul's passions, desires, affections, preventing these from being squandered on a thousand vain and transitory objects. Peace is the union and the fulfillment of all desires; and when the end of life is God Himself, infinitely good and therefore capable of satisfying and unifying the deepest and most diverse desires, peace becomes a reality. Here is the tranquillity of order which is the very essence of peace; the ordering of interior desires with tranquillity as the result. This is the "peace

(4) III. 15.
(5) I St. John. 4, 16.
(6) *Summa Theol.,* II II, 29, 3, c.

which surpasseth understanding," which "no man shall take from you."

3. The converse is also true. When men make creatures their end, rather than the Creator, their hearts will be pulled asunder and will not know peace. "But the wicked are like the raging sea, *which cannot rest.*" (7) Nor may we limit this truth (as is too often done by religious people, to the misfortune of the whole world) by saying that only those who are guilty of grave sin are deprived of peace, while all who avoid such sin, thus fulfilling the minimum requirements of God's law, although in other respects living for their own sensual enjoyment, can be said to direct their "feet into the way of peace." (8) We are to surrender our *whole* heart to God. The demand is for a total love, not for a certain measure of it, meted out with reluctance and complaining. True peace will be enjoyed in the proportion in which the demand for total love is satisfied.

"The love of God does not allow of any division in my heart. God is supremely jealous and wishes to possess it entirely, because He deserves it all; He will have it to Himself alone, because He alone deserves it, He has made it for no other than Himself, nor could He. If I turn the least of my affection away from Him to any creature in His place, I rob God of it; I take away from Him that which is His by every right, and which He will not give up to anyone else. I must love absolutely Himself alone, or, loving others, I must love them for Him, in reference to Him, because He wishes and as much as he wishes me to love them. In this way, all the affections of my heart will tend to Him as their End and Aim, and will all unite in Him as their Center. 'We do not love Thee enough, O my God,' says St. Augustine, 'if we love anything else with Thee, and not for Thee'." (9)

St. John of the Cross speaks in detail of five evils (two of which are relevant to the present subject and must be mentioned here) that will afflict a soul who, failing to love God

(7) Isa. 57, 20.
(8) St. Luke, 1, 79.
(9) Pere Grou, S.J., *Meditations on the Love of God*, 2nd Meditation. (London 1928: Burns, Oates.)

with that completeness which He deserves and demands, retains within itself "any disordered act of desire." Let us note first, too, that by a disordered act of desire is meant, not merely sinful desire—the saint is not speaking of sin in this place—but any desire or affection which is not centered in God and motivated by love for Him; in a word, any vain, selfish, sensual attachment for the creatures of this world, even though it does not reach the proportions of sin.

In the first place, he says, such desires "*weary* and *fatigue* the soul; for they are like restless and discontented children, who are ever demanding this or that from their mother and are never satisfied." (10) Clearly a soul that is wearied and fatigued is not at peace. Even when it has obtained its desire, it is still dissatisfied, according to the words of the Book of Job: "When he shall be filled, he shall be straitened, he shall burn, and every sorrow shall fall upon him." (11) "Which signifies: When he has satisfied his desire, he will be the more oppressed and straitened; the heat of desire hath increased in his soul and thus all grief will fall upon him." (12)

Secondly, these desires *torment* the soul and afflict it "after the manner of one who is in torment through being bound with cords from which he has no relief until he is freed." The saint gives another example to illustrate the same teaching: "And in the same way, wherein one that lies naked upon thorns and briars is tormented and afflicted, even so is the soul tormented and afflicted when it rests upon its desires. For they take hold upon it and wound and distress it and cause it pain, even as do thorns. Of these David says, 'They encompassed me about like bees, wounding me with their stings, and they are enkindled against me like fire among thorns'; (13) for in the desires, which are the thorns, the fire of anguish and torment increases." (14)

These truths, coming finally from divine revelation, are such as we can also test and prove by our own reflection and ex-

---

(10) *Ascent of Mt. Carmel*, Bk. I, Chap, 6, No. 6.
(11) Job 20, 22.
(12) St. John of the Cross, *op. cit.*
(13) Ps. 117, 12.
(14) St. John of the Cross, *ibid.*

perience: they are capable, if you will, of psychological as well as theological proof. A heart that is burdened by worldly cares and desires is restless and dissatisfied, wearied yet unable to find repose, envious, tortured, querulous, disquieted. Peace demands a purgation of the heart from all worldly dross. "The truth shall make you free": that is, the truth of Jesus Christ, which would have us renounce earthly affections and follow Him. This alone can rid us of the burden and the burning of desires that afflict the soul; it alone can cut the soul loose from the bonds that would otherwise keep it captive among sensual desires and lusts. And only when thus freed can the soul rise to that spiritual world where the Gifts of the Spirit (such as peace) are to be found and enjoyed. Meanwhile, the unspiritual man, the carnal man, he who is deliberately and resolutely imperfect—if he cannot even understand the things of God, (15) how can he hope to possess them? That which is holy is not given to dogs. And the dogs, as St. John of the Cross remarks, are those who, instead of loving God as He deserves, give their affections to creatures; for the children of God sit at table with Him and possess Him who is the Bread of life, while the dogs are those who reach out greedily for creatures, which are but crumbs of the divine goodness.

Spiritual activity having peace as its object must not be general and aimless. It must be definite and purposeful. "To nourish charity is to diminish worldly desire," St. Augustine said, "and where there is perfection of charity there will be no worldly desire." (16) It is the perfection of charity that the world wants when it asks for peace; it is therefore the destruction of worldliness and sensual affection for material goods that must be aimed at—and achieved!—if peace is in reality to be obtained.

Peace work should be carried forward, not by wordy discussions, but in the secret recesses of the human heart: in silence, in prayer, in meditation, in renunciation, and in all the spiritual exercises and practices that will clear the heart of whatever hinders it from being filled with love for God. The *immediate*,

(15) I Cor. 2, 14.
(16) Quoted from St. Thomas, *Summa Theol.*, II II, 24, 10.

practical procedure to be followed in any *realistic* effort to bring about peace (strange as it may appear even to Christian pacifists) is to make war on worldliness, vanity, egotism, love for riches and material goods, and on the tepidity and negligence that afflict even religious people. The manual of the pacifist should be a treatise on the spiritual life. His purpose and program should be that of earnest religious vowed to seek after perfection. The plan that he outlines for himself should be similar to that put before novices in fervent religious communities at the beginning of their religious life. The work and aim of the Christian pacifist, as a pacifist, does not differ from his work and aim as a Christian; it is by observance of the first and fundamental law of Christianity, that is, by his perfection as a Christian, that he will obtain peace.

4. The peace effort is really part of the Christian apostolate: it is coincident with that apostolate. One who loves God with his whole heart is a pacifist, a peacemaker; he is bringing supernatural peace into the world. Peace is therefore to be spread by means of the apostolate—an apostolate purified, supernatural in outlook and method, not relying in the first place on the clumsy and ineffective devices of human prudence. The peace movement must start out, not by political and economic programs or "points," but by the preaching and the practice of detachment, flight from the world, contempt of creatures, the pursuit of holiness. It must start in a word by inducing men to live in accordance with the teaching of the Gospel, always remembering that the latter is the "Gospel of peace." "We must strive"—wrote Benedict XV—"by every possible means to revive among men faith in the supernatural truths, and at the same time the esteem, the desire, and the hope of eternal goods. Your chief endeavors, Venerable Brethren, that of the clergy, and of all good Catholics, in their various societies, should be to promote God's glory and the true welfare of mankind. In proportion to the growth of this faith amongst men will be the decrease of that feverish striving after the empty goods of the world, and little by little, as brotherly love increases, social unrest and strife will cease." (17)

(17) *Ad Beatissimi.*

Evidently, then, Christian peace cannot be isolated from the rest of Christianity, nor sought after, as though it were an independent end, while ignoring other parts of Christian truth and practice. It can be enjoyed only through the practice of an integral Christianity. You cannot have the fruit unless you plant the tree; and peace is the fruit of love for God, which in turn is the substance and perfection of the Christian life. In a word, you do not really work for peace if you reject any of the high truths or austere obligations imposed on us by Jesus.

It will be said: "But what you ask is holiness of men; and this, for the mass of them, is impossible." It is indeed holiness that is needed; holiness alone can solve the world's problems. But it is not I, the writer of these words, who asks it, but God. It is God's law: "You shall be holy, for I am holy." (18) To say that holiness is impossible is to say that God is unjust.

Everywhere in the Scriptures peace and holiness, peace and righteousness, peace and justice (in the sense of sanctity) are linked together. St. Paul exhorts, "Follow after *peace* with all men *and holiness.*" (19) And again, "The kingdom of God is not in food and drink, but *righteousness and peace* and gladness in the Holy Spirit." (20) Long ages before, the Psalmist had summed up the matter perfectly: "I will hear what the Lord God will speak to me: for He will *speak peace* unto His people. And unto His *saints*: and unto them that are *converted to the heart.* . . . Mercy and truth have met each other: justice and peace have kissed." (21)

You desire peace? Desire to be a saint! Are you organizing to obtain peace? Then the first things to be cared for are the means which produce sanctity. Your political aims and economic plans can wait—second things should come second. The first thing is to pursue holiness. Say it is hard to go about it in this way, if you will. Only remember: if the word of God is to be credited, it is hopeless to attempt any other way.

---

(18) I St. Peter, I, 16.
(19) Heb. 12, 14.
(20) Rom. 14, 17.
(21) Ps. 84, 9-11.

IV

THE WAY TO SOCIAL PEACE

1. Let us now consider the second kind of peace, social peace, peace among men: how is it to be produced? We know already that it is a supernatural gift and the outward manifestation of inward peace. But there is still a practical question: How can this peace be made to take hold of and inform human relationships? As we have discovered and set down a procedure and method for obtaining interior peace, so must we also outline a definite procedure for seeking social peace. We must know what tasks to put our hands to, and in what order.

Both kinds of peace (it must be repeated, in order to take up the subject at the point to which we have come) involve a union of the appetites. Interior peace is essentially a union and quiescence of desires and appetites *within the soul;* and it is brought into existence by love of God. Social peace *presupposes* such interior repose in those who are party to it, but itself rather consists in a union of wills *among a number of men*; it is the concurrence of their desires, their unanimity in the choice of the great ends in life.

The question now is: what can effect a union of the wills of men living in society? What can bring their desires into harmony? Once again, the Angelic Doctor teaches, (1) it is charity; only, this time, the secondary activity of charity, love of neighbor. Love, indeed, is essentially a union of wills. Love of God is the union of man's will with God's; and this brings peace to the soul. Love of neighbor is a union of wills among men; and this brings peace to society.

Interior peace arises from obedience to the commandment to love God; social peace comes into existence through obedience to the commandment to love our neighbor as ourselves. The two kinds of peace correspond to the two obligations of charity. And as love for neighbor is simply the external and

(1) St. Thomas, *Summa Theol.*, II II, 29, 3, ad c.

practical manner of expressing love for God, since it regards and embraces Him in His visible human images, so in like manner social peace, proceeding from love of neighbor, is the outer expression of the inner peace that comes of love for God.

Why it is that social peace, while consisting essentially in a union of wills among men, presupposes also the repose of the desires within them, has already been explained in the preceding chapter. Wherever there is not such interior repose and union, at least in striving for the supreme object in life, conflicts will be inevitable, a union of wills and social peace impossible. The outward, political, union of men can be nothing other than the result and manifestation of their interior union in the search for God.

Peace, therefore, is as near to us as the First Commandment of God; but it is also, alas, as remote as the observance of that Commandment. If Christ has promised us peace, it is nevertheless only to come as a consequence of keeping the "new commandment" promulgated by Him. How useless to expect the gift of peace from Him if we do not obey the laws of supernatural life that operate to produce it! Will a farmer obtain the fruits he desires if he disregards the laws of nature in planting and cultivating his crops? The Church, in her official prayers for peace, *presupposes* this obedience to divine law: (2) "O God, from whom proceed holy desires, right counsels, and just works, grant to Thy servants that peace which the world cannot give; that, *our hearts having been dedicated to Thy commandments,* and the danger from our enemies being removed, our times through Thy protection may be peaceful."

2. Let it be remarked, too, that there is no short-cut to the love of neighbor. In our day there are some who mistakenly fancy that it can be attained without the love of God. It is a fatal delusion, responsible for nullifying all the fine talk of the modern world about the brotherhood of man. "Never perhaps was there more talking about the brotherhood of men than there is today; in fact, men do not hesitate to proclaim that striving after brotherhood is one of the greatest gifts of

(2) Collect of the Mass for Peace.

modern civilization, ignoring the teachings of the Gospel, and setting aside the work of Christ and of His Church. But in reality never was there less brotherly activity amongst men than at the present moment." (3) It is a sober fact that there is no other way of creating love among neighbors (and therefore peace) than by cultivating the love of God.

Cut the love of neighbor from its moorings in the love of God, and you have what we Americans love to call "service," that is, willingness to "love" and "serve" others as long as self interest finds it profitable to do so. Such "service," employed as a substitute for the charity of the Gospel, has in fact brought us back to the law and condition that obtained before the coming of the Gospel, namely: Love those that love you, hate those that hate you. Such is the law observed today. It is not the one whose observance brings peace.

Dutiful and affectionate children, genuinely concerned for the welfare of their parents and home, are united by this common love also to one another—the love of their parents creates peace among themselves. It is otherwise with children who do not love their parents: they are prone to regard family possessions jealously and selfishly, thus becoming divided among themselves. Similarly those who love God and place His interests above all else are united among themselves and enjoy peace. But those who have not love for God soon also become divided against each other over temporal goods.

St. Paul asserts the necessity of charity for peace when he says: "For all the law is fulfilled in one word: 'Thou shalt love thy neighbor as thyself.' But if you bite and devour one another, take heed you be not consumed one of another." (4) Whenever men keep the commandment of love—to paraphrase the saint—there will be peace; when they fail to keep it, they will consume one another. What a commentary is this text on what is proudly called global war! The world-wide rejection of Christ can have no other effect than world-wide destruction. Peace is measured by charity; hatred and discord, on the contrary, are in proportion to the violation of the Gospel

(3) *Ad Beatissimi.*
(4) Gal. 5, 15.

law. As our violation has been prolonged, unrepented, immense, so our wars can but be total and "global."

The Holy See has insistently reminded the modern world that charity is necessary if there is to be true peace. "Our Lord Jesus Christ came down from Heaven for the very purpose of restoring amongst men the Kingdom of Peace, which the envy of the devil had destroyed, and it was His will that it should rest on no other foundation than that of brotherly love. These are His own oft-repeated words: A new commandment I give unto you: That you love one another; This is my commandment that you love one another; These things I command you that you love one another; as though His one office and purpose was to bring men to mutual love." (5)

3. Furthermore, if the love of neighbor cannot flourish, or even exist, aside from love of God, so neither can it increase except through progress in Christian perfection and growth in holiness. Again, as progress in perfection and in love for God requires an emptying from the soul of merely earthly and carnal affections; as it requires a renunciation of *all things*, a renunciation to be accomplished at least in the heart; as it requires detachment from created goods and a preference for God over the things of earth—so also does love of neighbor, following from the love of God, demand the same virtues, the same renunciations, the same striving towards complete purity of heart. Newman defines holiness as "inward separation from the world." Not only does the commandment of love for God, which enjoins holiness and leads to it, demand such inward separation from the world; it is demanded as well by love of neighbor and peace among men.

Pope Pius XI explains the reason for this. "But it is of the very nature of material things that when sought unrestrainedly they bring with them every sort of evil, moral abasement and dissension first of all." (6) When men seek to lay up treasures on earth, then they envy one another, come into conflict in the pursuit of riches, become divided against each other, steal, murder. It is "of the very nature" of material goods to cause

(5) Benedict XV, *Ad Beatissimi.*
(6) *Ubi Arcano Dei.*

such dissensions! This is so because material goods are limited and cannot belong to more than one man simultaneously. Your wealth and affluence is a temptation to me, if I am worldly minded; and sooner or later our interests will conflict—unless, perhaps, we band together to take the possessions of someone else. Thus from the love of earthly goods come envy, dissension, enmity, quarreling, war.

Clearly, therefore, genuine love for God and detachment from the vanities of the world—at first sight so remote from the question of political peace—are in fact prerequisite for obtaining such peace. Do not men become rich by defrauding others of material goods, by robbing the laborer of his wages, by exploiting the poor and defenseless? It is precisely in this way that there arise industrial wars, class wars, international wars. The cure, obviously, lies in cultivating an attitude of soul which regards material goods with indifference and is able to use them unselfishly and for the glory of God.

The greater is the attachment to material goods, the more irreconcilable will be the divisions among men and the more furious their conflicts; as with pirates, the greedier they are, the more violent and murderous will be their assaults. "And further, as they [material goods] are confined within narrow limits the more they are shared the less there is for each. . . . Whence it comes that the things of the earth, inasmuch as they cannot satisfy all alike or fill the desires of anyone, become causes of discord and sickness of spirit. . . . And this comes on society as on individuals." (7)

Here is why wars get worse: their progress in destructiveness and horror is directly related to the increasing abandonment of divine law. It is not because of advances in science and technology—science and technology are but instruments—but rather because men, drifting further and further into forgetfulness of God, become at the same time more attached to the goods of earth. Ever more ruthless in their determination to secure these goods together with the paltry joys that come from them, they do not stop short of destroying whoever stands in the way of their satisfying themselves.

(7) Pius XI, *ibid.*

To carnal men, that is to those who pamper the desires of their fallen nature by pursuing the goods of earth, genuine supernatural love of neighbor is impossible. To such also peace is impossible. Spiritual goods become practical possibilities only when men mortify the flesh and live according to the Spirit. The very mark of the carnal man, St. Paul says, is that he does not observe the commandment of love: indeed, so closely is attachment to earthly goods connected with hatred and dissension that the Apostle defines the carnal man, not as one who seeks worldly joys, as we might expect, but rather as one who is divided against his neighbor. "For whereas there is among you envying and contention, are you not carnal. . . .?" (8) The carnal man, because he lives by a principle that divides him against others, simply cannot observe, or even comprehend, the commandment of loving one's neighbor. He may read it or recite it well enough; but he is like a man pronouncing the words of a tongue which he cannot understand. Because the world, despite the coming of Christ, remains carnal, it has neither known nor kept the new commandment by which the law of God is fulfilled. Hence while it has had periods of armistice it has never known peace.

4. It is almost automatically—as by law—that wars come from the love of material goods. Saying that war is a scourge from God for religious infidelity, is not to be taken as meaning that Almighty God chooses this kind of punishment rather than others and administers it personally or arbitrarily, as a father whips a disobedient child. Rather, when men neglect the first commandment of God, war follows inevitably, in the manner that certain effects follow necessarily from natural causes. War, a disease of society, takes hold of society in a manner similar to that in which physical disease takes hold of the body. When men abuse their bodies, we say that God punishes them. He does not intervene in any miraculous way to do this. But the bodily organs are made in accordance with certain physical laws, and if men for any reason violate or disregard these laws, then they are punished automatically by the diseases that follow from such abuses. The laws of nature operate even in

(8) I Cor. 3, 3.

their breach to punish those who do not observe them. Because the laws themselves come from God, we rightly say that it is God who punishes their violation.

Likewise God lays down certain moral and spiritual laws according to which men are to determine their conduct. When, however, they disobey these laws, moral disease and decay immediately appear. If men neglect God, it is because they have turned their hearts from Him to a merely sensual love for His creatures. In so doing, they put into motion the causes that will in due time mature in conflict and war. Through their pursuit of material riches they become divided against each other in the manner we have described; and the more ardent their pursuit, the more violent will be their collisions, for carnal men are "filled with all iniquity, malice, fornication, avarice, wickedness, full of envy, murder, contention." (9) In this way war comes from the violation of moral law; and because the law is from God, we rightly say that war is a punishment from God.

In our day these principles have a peculiar irony in that it was precisely through material goods that the false prophets of materialism thought that universal peace and prosperity were to be obtained. So proud of the ingenuity which, with the aid of science, created new inventions, produced them in great quantities, and opened up ever new sources of supply, these blind leaders of the blind boasted that through technical and material means mankind would attain to universal happiness. They saw in the developing systems of communication and transportation the means by which men were to be brought together in one universal brotherhood. In reality, however, the increase of wealth put men more furiously at one another's throats, caused class war and international conflicts, resulted everywhere in poverty, unemployment, and misery. The new developments in transportation and communication, as well as all the other marvelous inventions of science—railroads, gasoline engines, airplanes, radio, telephone, etc., etc.—became the very means by which the peoples of the earth locked them-

(9) Rom. 1, 29.

selves, not in the embrace of brotherhood, but in the most horrible slaughters that the world had ever seen.

The philosophers and scientists had perfected an ideal human society—without God. The only difficulty with it was that it did not work. God would not be excluded. Everywhere He was present in His world—despite the denials of the scientists—in His laws. And these laws, setting at naught human ingenuity and man's ability to control the forces of nature, were still strong enough, in their very breach, to topple all the grandiose plans of the new paganism for a "better" world. The first commandment of God, which requires that He be loved rather than creatures, was able, even in its universal violation —rather because of that violation—to bring down on our heads as deserved punishments the huge catastrophes of our day.

Were men to obey the injunction to "seek the things that are above," matters would be different. The love and pursuit of spiritual things would unite them and bring them peace. "... On the other hand, the things of the spirit, the more widely they are partaken of, enrich all without themselves ever diminishing." (10) If I give you five dollars, I become so much the poorer. But if I give you my knowledge—even all of it—I am none the poorer and you may now have more than I. In giving my knowledge to you, I actually increase my own, for the best way to learn is to teach. Such is the difference between material and spiritual goods. And of course spiritual goods include those of the supernatural order. In laboring to give others such grace or virtue as I possess, I do not decrease, but rather increase, my own spiritual treasures. In seeking to teach virtue to others, I strengthen the virtues of my own soul: in laboring to bring them grace, I add to the graces which I already possess.

Clearly, then, it would be possible, and even easy, if men were really to lay up treasures in heaven, to spread charity and peace among all men, and thus establish everywhere the kingdom of Christ, "a kingdom of justice, of love, and of peace." (11)

---

(10) *Ubi Arcano Dei.*
(11) Preface of Mass, Feast of Christ the King.

V

PUT YE ON THE LORD JESUS CHRIST

1. It is sometimes said by opponents of pacifism that, since the Gospels do not explicity forbid war or participation in it, the two are not incompatible. Indeed, the reason assigned by St. Augustine and St. Thomas for their teaching that there can be a just war is exactly this absence of any clear condemnation on the part of the Scriptures. (1) If war were evil by Christ's standards, then the Gospel should outlaw war and forbid the bearing of arms. Since, however, there is no such prohibition or condemnation in the Scriptures, it cannot be concluded (so it is said) that war is necessarily sinful or contrary to the Christian spirit.

While the possibility of just war has already been vindicated [and also shown to be a principle of pacifism rather than of militarism (1a)], it is nevertheless necessary to insist that St. Thomas's teaching should not be stretched any further than it was intended to go; his words must not be forced to mean something that they do not mean and were never intended to mean. What the Angelic Doctor holds is that war is not *intrinsically* evil. He does not, however, exclude the possibility of a war being *extrinsically* evil—evil, that is, by reason of its cause, its intention, the means by which it is waged. We must add, too, that when an action is extrinsically evil, it is still evil; and may well be quite as evil as a thing that is intrinsically evil. The view maintained here is that, even if war is not intrinsically evil, nevertheless in actual reality, it is almost always, if not always, extrinsically evil.

When it is said that war is not intrinsically evil, this means that, granted the necessary conditions, waging war does not of

(1) St. Thomas, *Summa Theol.*, II II, 40, 1, c.
(1a) See the Introduction.

itself, always, and necessarily involve sin. It means, at best and on the positive side, that war meets the standards of ethical righteousness. It does not yet mean, and cannot be forced to mean, that war accords with the spirit of the Gospel or that it is the means envisaged by the Gospel to establish justice and charity among men. There is a very important difference here, the whole difference between the natural and the supernatural orders. However excellent is natural law and justice, and however useful their study, the Christian may not stop with them, nor may he base his conduct on natural principles to the exclusion of the supernatural principles of Christ. To say that an action is not intrinsically evil means that it is in harmony with the natural law, or at any rate does not violate that law. It does not follow that such an action is prescribed, or recommended, or desired, or even envisaged by the Gospel. The absence of any condemnation in the Scriptures means at the most that war is not absolutely incompatible with salvation; it does not, however, establish that war, or participation in it, is the best means, or even a suitable means, for attaining salvation. In a word, it is a negative argument, not a positive demonstration; it is a permission, not an approval.

Elevated by grace to participation in the divine life, the Christian's conduct should henceforth be ruled by the double love of God and man; for "God is love." Having been, as it were, divinized, he is henceforth to be an "imitator of God." (2) "You were heretofore darkness, but now light in the Lord," St. Paul said to his converts; and he immediately draws the inescapable practical conclusion: "Walk then as children of the light." (3) If we are in truth "sons of God," (4) we can no longer measure our conduct by the norms of a merely natural righteousness, but only as befits sons of the most high God. Not the avoidance of gross sin, which is also demanded of the heathen, but the imitation of divine holiness, is the message of the Gospel. Only that is positively in accord with the Gospel spirit, therefore, which helps men to realize the divine ideal.

---

(2) Eph. 5, 1.
(3) Eph. 5, 8.
(4) St. John, 1, 12.

The standards of ethical righteousness, however excellent in their own order, are immeasurably lower than the standards of supernatural, or divine holiness.

Therefore, the final question to which the Christian must address himself is not, "Can war be ethically justified?" The main question is still before him; it is this: "Does war have a place in the way of life described by the Gospel? Is it to be the manner of settling differences among the members of the Mystical Body of Christ? Is it to have the same place of honor in the kingdom of God that it has had among barbarian nations? Above all, does the total war of today conform to the evangelic law of love?"

Now the teachings of St. Augustine and St. Thomas on the ethics of war do not answer this second question. Their doctrine must be taken as it is given: war is not intrinsically evil and may be *ethically* justified. The other, the more important question remains: "Is war Christ's way?" The Christian life—the manner in which all are called to conduct themselves in this world—is an imitation and reproduction of Christ's life. How does war and the killing of men, especially the mass slaughter of modern war, fit in with that pattern?

2. Therefore, if one asserts that war accords with the Gospel spirit, he cannot claim as support the traditional ethical doctrine concerning the possibility of a just war. The whole weight of his view rests on a merely negative argument, i.e., because war is not condemned in the Gospel of Jesus, it therefore fits into the pattern of life perfected by Him. This argument is called negative because it is not supported by any positive evidence in the New Testament but obtains whatever force it has from the absence of the opposite teaching. (4a)

Now negative arguments are of a very restricted value. At best they are but secondary and are useful chiefly to confirm and reinforce positive arguments. In the absence of positive argument not much weight can be placed upon them, and a

(4a) There are also positive arguments of course to demonstrate that war is not intrinsically evil—for example, the argument of reason (explained in the Introduction) and the divine sanction of war in the Old Testament. *There are, however, no positive arguments to prove that warfare is a desirable course of supernatural conduct.*

position that rests on merely negative proofs is far from unassailable. Thus it might be argued negatively that, because monopolies are not condemned in the Constitution of the United States, they are not incompatible with American ideals; yet, in fact, monoplies and the evils they bring are among the forces chiefly responsible for defeating the American ideal of democracy. So also, to take an example in the matter of religion, it might be argued negatively, as certain heretics do argue, that since infant Baptism is not commanded in the Scriptures, it is therefore not prescribed by the divine law. Yet the Catholic Church requires parents, under pain of sin, to present their children for Baptism as soon as possible after birth. In other words, for the Church, the positive indications of the necessity of Baptism outweigh the merely negative argument.

Hence, although we accept the traditional ethical teaching within the limits of its meaning, the conclusion does not follow that war accords with the ideal of life described by the Gospel or is in agreement with the Spirit of Christ. The silence of the Scriptures on this point cannot be construed as an argument in favor of war, *even of just war*. The Gospel is silent on many questions which have nevertheless been solved in time through principles taught in the Gospels.

Slavery is an example of an institution likewise not explicitly forbidden by Christ, therefore not intrinsically evil, yet gradually disappearing under the influence of His teaching. Slavery is not intrinsically evil, hence it is not forbidden by the New Testament. No less a person than St. Paul acquiesces in it when he bids slaves be subject to their masters. (5) He even returned a runaway Christian slave to his master Philemon.

Nevertheless, we rightly attribute the disappearance of slavery to the leavening influence of Christianity. And it is remarkable that St. Paul, in the very act of returning the slave Onesimus to his owner, appealed to a law and set down a principle that was ultimately to destroy slavery. He appealed to the law of love: "*For charity's sake,*" he said, "I rather beseech thee for *my son*, whom I have begotten in bonds, Onesimus . . . and do thou receive him *as my own heart* . . . [Receive him]

(5) Col. 3, 32.

not now as a servant, but instead of a servant, *a most dear brother,* especially to me: but how much more to thee both in the flesh and in the Lord." (6) The Apostle here deliberately lays aside justice and appeals to the law of love; this law compelled masters to treat their slaves, no more as chattel, but as brothers and sons. Christian charity destroyed precisely that element in slavery which made it profitable, and thus undermined the foundations of the whole pagan economic system. Thus did Christianity work in the secret recesses of history to bring to an end an evil that seemed to be part of society itself —without which, as it appeared even to good and holy men, society could not exist and would simply collapse.

Is it too much to hope that the same law of love, still at work in history, can destroy another slavery, more intolerable than that of old, the slavery by which the common people are defrauded of their goods, their vocation, their very lives, and are trained to murder their fellow-poor—and all this for no other purpose than to obtain or protect raw materials and markets and colonies and "spheres of influence"?

There is no need of an explicit condemnation of war in the Scriptures. The law of love, the great law of the Gospels, is opposed to it, as it was to slavery, and will eventually triumph over it. This law requires men to love their enemies, just as masters were required to love their slaves. It is love therefore that can dissolve the enmity and hatred of which war is the outward expression. Love requires us to see in our enemies, not the monsters that war-time propaganda makes of them, but our brothers in Jesus Christ, redeemed by His blood, sons of God even as ourselves. Do men murder their brothers? Cain did But it is Christ, not Cain, who is the exemplar for Christians.

3. In the life of Jesus we find a perfect illustration of the law of love in action and of what is meant by living a divine life on earth. This law and this life should determine the attitudes and conduct of Christians in the matter of war as in all other matters. Alas, large numbers of men today act as though war had no spiritual implications whatsoever, as though there

(6) Philemon 1.

were no law of love. Their relish of fighting, their hatred of "enemies"; their glorying in arms and the merely military virtues; their refusal, or failure, to see anything objectionable in wholesale destruction and slaughter; their readiness to condone as "military necessities" all the horrors and cruelty of modern war; their callous refusal to be affected by the sufferings engendered by war—in all this they think and act exactly "as those who know not God." If we go to the example of Christ—rather than to the practice of reprisal which is the only principle accepted by modern warring nations—we will have some difficulty in understanding the views of such persons and in reconciling with the profession of Christianity a positive enthusiasm for the deeds of blood that mark the history of "Christian" peoples down to the present day.

Is this record of blood, this slaughter of the innocent, this frightful oppression of the poor and helpless—tearing them from their homes, teaching them to kill and to be killed, depriving them of those "inalienable rights" which we profess to belong to all men—is all this in accordance with the merciful plans of the Prince of Peace? Does the Christian conscience find nothing to object to in the increasing cruelty and horror of modern warfare? Can it view without alarm what Pope Pius XII called "the most formidable, destructive and devastating war of all time"? Not so the Holy Father, the authentic voice of the Christian conscience, who thus answers the question whether war, especially that of today, is compatible with the Gospel: "In all nations aversion is growing against the brutality of the methods of total war, *which goes beyond all just limits, all rules of divine and human right.* More than ever the minds and hearts of peoples are tormented by doubt whether continuation of such a war can be in accordance with national interest, *or reasonable and justifiable before Christian and human conscience.*" (7)

Again, if we take Christ's conduct as our norm, what shall we think of the opinion of those who say that war is, after all, good for the people; that suffering is useful and war gives to

(7) Address on the Fourth Anniversary of the beginning of World War II, Sept. 1, 1943.

men a taste of the cross; that as Christians we cannot share that weakly, sentimental sympathy for suffering which characterizes humanitarianism. Such views, it goes without saying, are urged usually by those who do not themselves share in the sufferings brought by war, just as the duty of going to war is most eloquently defended by those who are able to excuse themselves from discharging that duty. Yet aside from this fact, what shocking cynicism is revealed in this outlook, what ignorance of the virtues enjoined by the Gospel. Did not Christ "have compassion on the multitudes"? Shall we then do less? Did He not show a wonderful sympathy for human suffering, going among the lame, the halt, the blind, in order to cure them of their diseases and relieve them of their pain? Was it mere sentimentality or humanitarianism that caused Him to do so? If, however, it was divine love, as indeed it was, that prompted His conduct, then certainly the humanitarians should be congratulated for having learned at least this much from the Teacher whom they reject, while we in turn ought to be ashamed when, professing to be the followers of Christ, we have not learned even this most elementary lesson of Christian love and compassion.

The very definition of a Christian life is to conduct one's self as Christ conducted Himself. The rule which the saints, following this principle, give for meeting all the problems of life is to ask ourselves, "How would Christ meet this situation? What, then, is the Christ-like thing for me to do?" Now apply this rule, not merely to the general view of war, but to the concrete circumstances in which those involved in war find themselves. Can you think of Christ dropping bombs on helpless cities? Can you think of Him slaughtering with all the devices of scientific mass murder women, children, non-combatants? Can you think of Him as engaging in, or condoning as a military necessity, the frightful barbarities that are the ordinary procedure of modern war? Can you think of Him using these cruel methods Himself, as an act of duty, performing them in accordance with His undeviating principle of doing the Father's will? Can you think of Jesus maiming and killing the poor conscripts—on whatever side they might be—

who are forced unwillingly to be soldiers by the all-powerful State? Can you think of Him inciting men to hatred, or acquiescing in hatred in the name of patriotism? Can you think of Him participating in the "commando tactics" and in the other brutalities that form part of the modern soldier's training? Can you think of Him saying, "It is necessary to do these things, no matter how regrettable in themselves, if we are to win"? Can you think of His making the physical survival of any group the supreme law?

If you believe that war is in accordance with the Gospel, *it should be possible to answer all these questions affirmatively.* You should be able to think of Christ in any situation into which soldiers are compelled to go today and carrying out all orders that such soldiers are given by those in authority. You must be able to think of how Christ would act as a gunner or a bombardier; of His carrying out the murderous order to take no prisoners; of His destroying cities, strafing troops, killing them indiscriminately without regard for moral guilt; of His leveling factories which hold thousands of workers whose crime is the desire for work and whose need for bread is used by modern states to force them into supporting the war system; of His destroying great projects, like factories or dams, thereby to cause the death of non-combatants and ruin utterly the results of generations of labor and industry. If you cannot think of Christ doing these things, then war stands condemned by the Christian conscience. For every man, every soldier, is bound by duty to the imitation of Christ; in the performance of any duty, he should ask himself, and should be free to ask himself: "How would Jesus do this? What is the Christ-like thing to do?" Any system in which men are not free to ask that question, and answer it, and do what their Christian conscience enjoins, stands condemned before God.

In conclusion, try to imagine Jesus Christ among the men described in the following report from the front. Here in the concrete is what war does to men. Ask yourself whether this conduct can be fitted into the pattern of Christian life.

I was away from the front lines for a while this spring, living with other troops, and considerable fighting took place while I was gone. When I got ready to return to my old friends at the front, I wondered if I would sense any change in them.

I did, and definitely.

The most vivid change is the casual and workshop manner in which they now talk about killing. They have made the psychological transition from the normal belief that taking human life is sinful, over to a new professional outlook where killing is a craft. To them now, there is nothing morally wrong about killing. In fact, it is an admirable thing. . . .

But to the fighting soldier, that phase [i.e., the moral repugnance to killing] of the war is behind. It was left behind after his first battle. His blood is up. He is fighting for his life, and killing now for him is as much a profession as writing is for me.

He wants to kill individually or in vast numbers. He wants to see the Germans overrun, mangled, butchered in the Tunisian trap. He speaks excitedly of seeing great heaps of dead, of our bombers sinking whole shiploads of fleeing men, of Germans by the thousands dying miserably in a final Tunisian holocaust of his own creation.

Is it possible to think that the men described by this reporter (8) are, in their lives, obeying the Apostle's injunction to "put on the Lord Jesus Christ"? (9) Is it by learning to regard murder as a craft that millions of men are to fulfill their Christian vocation?

---

(8) The reporter was Ernie Pyle. Syndicated article, April 22, 1943.
(9) Rom. 13, 14.

VI

BLESSED ARE THE PEACEMAKERS

1. While John the Baptist was preaching one day, some soldiers "also asked him, saying: What shall we do? And he said to them: Do violence to no man; and be content with your pay." (1) These words of the great precursor are frequently cited to show that soldiering (and therefore war) are not incompatible with evangelical holiness; for, if they were, then certainly John would have been obliged to tell these inquirers to put aside their weapons and change their calling. Actually he told them simply to be satisfied with the pay they were getting and not to supplement it by plundering others. Apparently, then, he saw nothing objectionable in their profession, which, it would seem, he accepted as a legitimate vocation. The incident seems to bear out the contention that no positive teaching in the Gospels discountenances war. Here indeed is a text that seems even to acquiesce in it.

However, careful study reveals more in this Scriptural incident than first meets the eye; and, at the most, no more can be concluded from it than that war may be ethically justified: at most it allows the conclusion that war is not evil in itself and in every conceivable case; that is, intrinsically evil. The words of John still leave open and unanswered the question of what the positive teaching of the Gospel is in regard to war, i.e., whether it enjoins or approves of war. St. Augustine used this text in support of his thesis that there can be a just war; it illustrates his saying that the Scriptures do not condemn war as evil. It proves no more than this; it does not prove that warfare positively accords with the Gospel spirit.

Mark: St. John the Baptist did not simply tell the soldiers to be content with their pay. He told them also to "do violence to no man." Rather a remarkable counsel to address to a soldier! It is to tell him that, of course, he may go on sol-

(1) St. Luke, 3, 14.

diering but he is not to engage in that activity which chiefly characterizes soldiers. It is something like encouraging a boy to become a scholar while forbidding him to read any books; or like giving him permission to go for a swim but forbidding him to get wet. The new English translation of the Bible changes the wording of St. John's exhortation somewhat. According to this version he said, "Plunder no one . . ." There is however no contradiction between the two translations; they complement one another, and we will probably come closest to the Baptist's meaning, as contained in the Greek text, when we take both together. The two ideas—of plundering and of violence—are contained in the words used both by the Latin translation and the Greek original, and that of violence is certainly dominant.

This means that St. John, while not discountenancing soldiering as a profession, limits its duties to those of policing. (1a) Actually, in John's day, when the *Pax Romana* was spread throughout the known world, the Roman soldier was in fact a kind of international policeman. The saint's words can best be understood in relation to the situation for which he was legislating; they must be interpreted with reference to the men to whom they were as a matter of fact addressed. They should not be taken, without such precautions, as universal teaching in regard to war. In the very act of accepting the status of these soldiers, St. John definitely limits its functions; and what he eliminates is precisely what is objectionable and incompatible with the religious conscience. He allows for the need of policemen to keep order (as does the Christian pacifist), but he prohibits violence and destruction and injustice.

Thus, it appears that in answering the question addressed to him, St. John did not contemplate war on a larger, national or international scale; what he wished to use his influence to correct was the private pillaging by brutal and unscrupulous soldiers of a subject population. This is the situation that he actually saw; it is to be presumed then that it was the situation

(1a) Another way to state the matter is to say that the saint did not condemn soldiering *as such*—a phrase whose meaning and limits have been explained in the Introduction. *In the concrete*, however, he requires that soldiers make a definite and remarkable change in their behavior.

that he was trying to change. In this event, his words have no relevance to the greater problem of war at all; and assuredly he did not envisage the horrors of total and scientific warfare. His contemporaries were not as enlightened as we are; the Romans, for all their cruelty, or even the ferocious barbarians without the Empire, could not dream of duplicating the hideous destruction that is the daily routine of twentieth century war. But even if we take his words to apply to war in the larger sense, no more can be concluded from them than from the objection considered in the preceding chapter, namely, that war is not intrinsically evil.

2. It must also be observed that these are the words of John the Baptist; not of Christ. Although "there hath not risen among them that are born of women a greater than John the Baptist," nevertheless "he that is the lesser in the kingdom of God is greater than he." (2) John's teaching can scarcely be taken as fully representative of a Gospel that had not yet even been preached. His message, which was part of his mission, could go no further than the mission itself: it could be no more than a preparation for the Gospel. Whatever John's holiness or gift of prophecy, it was not given him to reveal the fully matured teaching of Jesus.

If we wish to know the Gospel teaching, we must go to the Gospel. Here we find, not silence in regard to the problem of war, as is so often supposed and stated, but an explicit manifestation of God's will. In the seventh Beatitude Christ said, "Blessed are the peacemakers, for they shall be called the children of God." In view of these words, it is difficult to understand the assertion that there is nothing in war incompatible with Christianity. What could be clearer or more direct than this? In the very Beatitudes, which have a special importance among the sayings of Jesus, is this praise, not only of peace, but of peace*making*. Christians are called not simply to enjoy, but to make peace: this is to be an important characteristic of their special religious activity.

If all Christ's utterances are oracles of Him who is the Truth, these Beatitudes enjoy a special preeminence because they

(2) St. Matt. 11, 11.

summarize the most essential features of the divine pattern of living which our Lord imposed on all mankind in the Sermon on the Mount. They comprise, in fact, the Christian Manifesto to the world. Why is it that eight particular acts and practices are singled out from all the other elements of the Christian life for a special blessing and beatitude? Because, answers the Angelic Doctor, they are peculiarly well fitted to bring men to their eternal beatitude and indeed give them already in this life some beginning and share in supernatural blessedness. (3) Peacemaking is one of the actions so singled out and blessed by Jesus. The last, the culminating Beatitude reveals that His followers are to be, not warriors, but peacemakers.

Indeed, not only is beatitude attached to peacemaking, but even the highest beatitude. For, as St. Thomas teaches, the rewards attached to the several Beatitudes are stated in a cumulative order (4); each adds something new to the promise contained in the previous one. Thus, as a Christian passes from one Beatitude to the next, he merits increasingly great spiritual privileges. The possession of eternal goods in security and tranquillity, which is promised in the second Beatitude, is better than merely holding or having such goods, as is promised in the first; for we may have many things of which we do not have firm possession. It is still better to enjoy consolation among the goods of eternity, as is promised in the third Beatitude, than it is both to have them and possess them; sometimes possession brings but sorrow. Again, to be filled with abundance of consolation, as the fourth Beatitude pledges, is better than simply to be consoled, just as it is better to have the fullness of knowledge than merely some knowledge. The fifth Beatitude adds still more when it promises mercy; for this means that those who accept Christ's law will be filled, not according to their own deserts, which would be very limited, but according to the infinite mercy of God. The sixth contains the promise to see God, and this is more wonderful still, as it is a greater honor to live with a king and enjoy his

(3) *Summa Theol.*, I II, 69, 2, c.
(4) *Ibid* I II,, 69, 4 and 3.

presence than it is to enjoy plenty in his court but at a distance from his person. The next reward, the climactic promise (4a) of Our Lord, is granted to the peacemakers: "They shall be called the children of God." Not only shall they see God, but, being adopted by Him as sons, they come to resemble Him in holiness, as children resemble their parents, thereby entering in the most intimate way into His love.

Who are these peacemakers to whom so glorious a privilege is extended? Those, replies St. Thomas, who make peace either in themselves or in others. (5) What is this peace? That has already been answered: "Let the *peace of Christ* rejoice in your hearts. (6) How are men to *make* this peace? In accordance with the axiom of modern statesmanship, "If you wish peace, prepare for war"? By military victory? By guns and airplanes and bombs? This is the way in which the men of the world set out to make "peace." The Christian, however, works in a different manner. Knowing that peace is the act and effect of love, he knows also that it can be made only through the use of those spiritual means which increase divine love in the soul.

3. To realize as fully as possible the force and meaning of the seventh Beatitude, we must grasp its connection with the others and also with the whole Sermon on the Mount. The fundamental idea, or theme, of this Sermon is that henceforth men are not to act like mere human beings, following the inclinations of their fallen nature as the heathens do, but, having been divinized by grace, they are to act as divine beings, seeking after the things of God. "Lay not up to yourselves treasures on earth where the rust and the moth consume and where thieves break in and steal. But rather lay up to yourselves treasures in heaven where neither rust nor moth consumes and where thieves do not break in nor steal." (7) Dead to the world, living only for God, Christians are expected to live their lives in the world of the divine. "Mind the things that are

---

(4a) The eighth Beatitude, following that of the peacemakers, summarizes the others, and refers to all of them.

(5) *Summa Theol.*, II II, 45, 6, c.

(6) Col. 3, 15.

(7) St. Matt. 6, 19-20.

above, not the things that are on earth. For you have died, and your life is hidden with Christ in God." (8)

The Beatitudes take this fundamental theme and make it more concrete, giving it specific applications. The first three show that true happiness is to be obtained only by putting aside mere earthly or human happiness, the happiness of mere pleasure as St. Thomas calls it; (9) the last five describe in particular the supernatural and divine conduct that will be from now on expected of Christians.

The first Beatitude shows that happiness is to be achieved through poverty of spirit, that is through the exterior renunciation of external goods, like money and reputation. This means that, to find true happiness, the soul must free itself from precisely that thing in whose possession the vast majority of men wrongly think to find happiness. So also do the second and third Beatitudes bless, not the possession, but the privation of the several remaining varieties and classes of earthly goods. The second promises happiness to those who are deprived of the pleasures and comforts of the body; it condemns those who seek such goods: "Blessed are you who hunger now, for you shall be satisfied. . . . Woe to you who are filled! for you shall hunger." The third blesses those who are deprived of earthly joy, condemns those who pursue it: "Blessed are you who weep now, for you shall laugh. . . . Woe to you who laugh now! for you shall mourn and weep." (10)

The fourth Beatitude fixes the positive supernatural end for all Christians, the final goal which is henceforth to be the object of their efforts: "Blessed are they who hunger and thirst for justice." Because justice obliges us to return what is due, not only to our fellow men, but also and above all to God, it fixes our great object in life as righteousness or holiness. The just man praised in the Scriptures is not he who practices social justice in the sense in which we understand that term today, (11) but rather he who lives his whole life in accordance with

---

(8) Col. 3, 1-3.
(9) *Beatitudo voluptuosa. Summa Theol.*, I II, 69, 3, c.
(10) St. Luke, 6, 21-25.
(11) See Psalm 1.

the standard established by God. The goal of human life is therefore not any kind of earthly goods, even those of the mind, but holiness. And since holiness is first of all a divine attribute, rather than a quality belonging properly to men, Jesus, in commanding us to be holy, is telling us to be as God: "For the grace of God our Saviour hath appeared to all men, instructing us, that, denying ungodliness and worldly desires, we should live soberly, and justly, *and godly* in this world." (12)

4. Herewith a merely human ideal of righteousness, such as was known under the Old Law, and is known even to the heathens, is done away with. Now "the faithful soul should make its effort to model itself as much as possible on the divine ways. . . . For the more it has been modeled on its Creator in this world, the more it will be like Him in the life to come, and the more it is like Him, the greater will be its bliss, the more it will give glory to God and will be useful to every creature." (13)

Set down as a general proposition in the fourth Beatitude, this great truth is further elucidated in those following. Men are to be merciful. Why? Because God is merciful. They are to be clean of heart, that is, inwardly pure in their hearts and desires, just as God is wholly pure; they are not to be satisfied with a mere external respectability such as is acceptable to men. For the same reason, finally, we are to be peacemakers. God is a peacemaker and we are to be as He is. "For indeed," St. Thomas remarks, "to create peace in one's self or in others is to show one's self an imitator of God, who is the God of unity and peace." (14)

Within God, among the Persons of the Trinity, because infinite love unites them, there is eternal and undisturbed harmony and peace. And Jesus, in bidding men to love one another, desires this that they may be the children of their Father who is in heaven. (15) Thus by love we come to be like Him who is love; by love we come to resemble the "God of Peace"

---

(12) Tit. 2, 11-12.

(13) St. Thomas, *The Ways of God.* (The Spiritual Classics Series, Christian Culture Press, Assumption College, Windsor, Canada). Page 38.

(14) *Summa Theol.*, I II, 69, 4, c.

(15) St. Matt. 5, 45.

(16), able then both to share and diffuse His peace. Love at one and the same time makes us peacemakers (i.e., pacifists) and children of God. By peacemaking we come to resemble God; by striving to resemble God we inevitably become peacemakers. Thus does the law of evangelic love and the duty of pursuing holiness bring us to the supernatural pacifism of Christ. What further evidence is needed to show that the Gospel is opposed to divisions, hatred, contention among men, as also to the concrete expression of these evils in war?

Of course men come to resemble God through imitating the Son of God, Jesus Christ. So that it is the seventh Beatitude which, besides making men peacemakers (and in the very fact that it makes them peacemakers), perfects their resemblance to Jesus. In the seventh Beatitude, as in each of the others, two elements may be distinguished: (17) an element of merit, which is the particular action designated as specially meritorious for obtaining eternal blessedness (i.e., "Blessed are the poor in spirit"); secondly, the element of reward, which is the special felicity attached in each case to the desirable action (i.e., "for theirs is the kingdom of heaven"). In the seventh Beatitude, both parts bring the soul to the most intimate union and imitation of God. The first part, the element of merit ("Blessed are the peacemakers"), makes us, as we have seen, imitators of God, while the second part, promising that we shall be children of God, shows us that this divine resemblance, perfected by peacemaking, is to be accomplished through conformity to Christ. "Now these are called the children of God" —says St. Thomas in commenting on this Beatitude—"in so far as they share the likeness of the only begotten and natural Son of God." (18)

The reward of peacemaking is sonship with the Father and resemblance to the Son—the fulfillment of the whole purpose of Christian life. It is Christ who gives us the example of how to live a divine life in the world. As He was perfect in all things, the fullest possible realization of what the Father intended human life to be like, so does He illustrate perfectly

(16) Phil. 4, 9.
(17) *Summa Theol.*, I II, 69, 2.
(18) *Ibid.*, II II, 45, 6, c.

the activity of peacemaking, so agreeable to the Father. (19) Others who would be sons of God are truly His sons in the degree of their resemblance to this Only Begotten Son: those whom God "foreknew, He also predestinated to be made conformable to the image of His Son; that He might be the first-born among many brethren." (20) It is the Beatitude of the Peacemakers that shows how this resemblance is to be perfected and its culminating felicity obtained.

---

(19) In Chapter X we will consider Jesus in the role of Peacemaker.
(20) Rom. 8, 29.

VII

A NEW COMMANDMENT . . . .

1. A new question, urgent and important, arises at once from the doctrine explained in the preceding chapter. What, precisely is the obligation imposed by the Beatitudes? Is there any? May they be treated, as the entire Sermon on the Mount is so often treated, as indeed containing a sublime ideal of action, but not demanding strict obedience from all? As helpful for those generous souls who aspire to sanctity, but not intended for the rank and file of men?

In order to grasp the problem fully, it is necessary to bear in mind the distinction ordinarily made between two types of divine ordinances: precepts or commandments, like "Thou shalt keep holy the Sabbath day," which bind under pain of sin; and counsels, which are a recommendation by God of certain optional courses of conduct, highly desirable but not necessary. The three great counsels recognized by traditional Christian teaching are poverty, chastity, and obedience. Members of religious communities recognize the force and value of these counsels by freely vowing to observe one or more of them; but lay people, to whom sanctity and salvation are also open, have no obligation to follow them. All Christians, then, are bound by the precepts; only those specially called and voluntarily binding themselves are required to follow the higher way of the counsels.

The nature of the problem and its practical implications should now be apparent. If the Beatitudes are only counsels, then, however admirable they may be, their observance is not obligatory; individuals and nations incur no guilt in disregarding them. Moreover, they are in fact frequently regarded as counsels; so that even Catholics are not indignant when specifically Christian standards of conduct are violated in national policies. Nothing else can be expected of secular governments and non-Catholic peoples, it is said; if these were to conform simply to the law of nature, this would be sufficient to end war and bring real peace. Accordingly, in the demands stipulated by Catholics for realizing a just peace, you find them basing their programs on the law of nature, often without mention of the Gospel teaching. No doubt the framers of these programs will say that their plans are concerned only with the minimum requirements. But may we be satisfied with any arrangement that neglects the Gospel and the greatest commandment of God?

You see, therefore, the importance of the subject. The attitude that we should take towards war hinges on the question whether the Beatitude of the Peacemakers should be understood as preceptive or of counsel only.

As a matter of fact it is neither. The Beatitudes are simply actions—highly meritorious actions, which, proceeding from the supernatural virtues and the Gifts of the Holy Spirit, are of special value in bringing men to supernatural happiness. (1) They are not themselves virtues or commands or even counsels, and they do not therefore carry any special obligation of their own. In a word, the Eight Beatitudes are not so much a code of Christian legislation as a description and epitome of those acts which are especially to be desired and commended in Christians and are of particular value to them in seeking for their eternal salvation.

This is not to say that there is no obligation attached to the Beatitudes, that there is no compulsion. But it means that whatever obligation they have proceeds from the virtues which they in a unique manner express; and the kind and degree of their obligation is to be discovered by attending to the virtues to which they respectively belong. For example, the first Beatitude is an act of the virtue of poverty; its place and importance in the Christian life is therefore to be known through a just appreciation of this virtue.

From what virtue, then, proceeds the Beatitude of the Peacemakers? Knowing this we can measure the urgency of the duty it imposes. The question has already been answered. Peace is an act and effect of the virtue of charity; it binds us

(1) St. Thomas, *Summa Theol,* I II, 69, 1, c.

therefore in the manner that charity binds. Is there any need to ask the manner of this obligation? Charity is "the greatest and first commandment"; (2) it is "the fulfilling of the law." (3) Christian pacifism derives from the central and essential obligation of Christianity. There is no doctrinal ground for treating it as icing.

More: if Christians are in fact to be Peacemakers, they must practice charity in a very eminent degree. For the Beatitudes are not only acts of the virtues, but, according to St. Thomas, they are acts of perfect virtue. (4) To be a Peacemaker one should seek the perfection of love. When men are ruled habitually by divine love; when love for God and not for themselves or for the creatures of the world is the dominating passion of their lives—then will they be Peacemakers.

This conclusion is confirmed in another manner. As both St. Thomas and St. Augustine show, each Beatitude is related in a special way to one of the Gifts of the Holy Spirit; so that each of the actions described in the Beatitudes may be said to be performed under the influence of its corresponding Gift. Poverty of Spirit, for example, is practiced especially with the help of the Gift of Fear of the Lord, the reason being that this Gift causes the soul to distrust and fear its own weakness and sinfulness, and therefore to practice great detachment and humility.

Peacemaking, St. Thomas teaches, is practiced especially under the impulse of the Gift of Wisdom. Now even among the Gifts there is a kind of hierarchy, some caring for more elementary spiritual needs, others coming into play only later on, at more advanced stages of spiritual development. Thus Knowledge, one of the more "elementary" Gifts, teaches the soul the emptiness of the world and the contempt for creatures, a lesson which must be learned at the threshold of spiritual living, otherwise the soul can never go further. Wisdom, however, is the highest of the Gifts because it introduces the soul into the closest union and conformity with God that is possible to men in this world. And Peacemaking, we say, belongs

(2) St. Matt. 22, 38.
(3) Rom. 13, 10.
(4) *Summa Theol.*, II II, 29, 4 ad 1.

especially to the Gift of Wisdom and is perfected as this Gift comes into play and exerts its influence on the soul. (5) Peacemaking thus belongs to the character of the *complete* Christian; to the fullness and maturity of the Christian life.

If you would know the reason for this association of Wisdom and Peacemaking, it follows from what has already been said. By Peacemaking we are conformed to Christ; and Christ is "the Truth," (6) the very Wisdom of God, the Word Made Flesh. It is by sharing in the divine Wisdom that conformity to Christ is effected in our souls and we become in truth "sons of God." Since peacemaking is so powerful to bring about a likeness to Jesus, it must be in a special way related to the Gift that works to perfect the same likeness.

Furthermore, this same Gift of Wisdom, St. Thomas teaches, introduces the soul into the higher degrees of prayer and special intimacy with God. Thus, no matter from what angle you view the subject, Peacemaking is always to be found near the summit of Christian perfection. By Peacemaking you will reach this summit; in scaling this summit you will become a Peacemaker. Peace, it is clear, is a higher thing than is suspected by the politicians, editors, and humanitarian reformers who talk most fluently about it. No wonder St. Ignatius of Antioch exclaims, "There is nothing better than peace, by which every war in heaven and on earth is abolished!" (7) You see how useless it is for the world to seek peace without Christ? To promote peace plans based on only natural law?

Mark, too, that not only love, but *the perfection of love,* falls under *the precept.* "Thou shalt love the Lord thy God with thy *whole* heart. . . ." "The love of God and neighbor does not fall under the precept to a certain extent only, so that whatever is above this may be said to be merely of counsel. This is evident from the very form of the precept which implies totality and perfection: 'Love the Lord thy God with thy *whole* heart.' For totality and perfection are the same thing, as the Philosopher also remarks." (8) The love that is demanded by

(5) *Ibid.*, II II, 45, 6, c.
(6) St. John 14, 6.
(7) *Letter to the Ephesians.*
(8) St. Thomas, *Summa Theol.*, II II, 184, 3 c.

the precept is absolute, exclusive, total. "Thus the perfection of divine love falls under the precept universally, so that even the perfection which is attained only in heaven is not excluded." (9)

2. With these truths in mind it is easy to meet the objections to pacifism which are based on the distinction between the precepts and the counsels. In dispensing ourselves from the counsels, let us be careful that we do not attempt to throw aside any of the precepts; above all, let us not throw out the precept of love. This is what happens to those who use this distinction without understanding its meaning. It is said, for example, that "Do not resist evil," (10) or "Turn the other cheek," (11) or "Revenge not yourselves . . . but give place unto wrath," (12) and other similar injunctions in the Scriptures, are counsels only and therefore carry no strict obligation with them. Sometimes (it will be added, with truth) it is not possible to observe the counsels; as when a father is bound by duty to defend his home or a Bishop his flock and the interests of the Church. Moreover, both St. Augustine and St. Thomas knew these texts but did not think that they contradict their teaching concerning the possibility of a just war.

By all means let us call such Scriptural exhortations counsels: they recommend a higher course of conduct which is not always possible or permissible. But do not forget that although *these counsels* do not bind under pain of sin, and their observance is sometimes limited and even prevented by actual circumstances, on the other hand *the Gospel law and precepts* bind all men to obedience. The fact that the counsels do not apply in certain cases can never be a reason for throwing out the precepts. Yet this is exactly what happens when it is forgotten that love, and the perfection of love, is not a counsel but a precept. Because certain things in the Gospel are of counsel only, this seems to be sufficient reason for some to discard altogether the Gospel and its precepts as irrelevant or not of binding force. The baby is thrown out with the bath

(9) *Ibid.*, II II, 184, 3 ad 2.
(10) St. Matt. 5, 39.
(11) St. Luke 6, 29.
(12) Rom. 12, 19.

water, and the problem of war (among others) is then solved by merely natural principles of ethics without reference to the ethics of Christ.

The precepts of the Gospel, over and above those of the natural law and the Mosaic code, constitute *a law* that seriously binds all men and nations. This law has many applications but is summed up in the command to love God above all things and our neighbor as ourselves; "for love therefore is the fulfillment of the law." (13) Once and for all this commandment determines the proper *end* of the Christian life: union with God through the fullness of love. The counsels, on the other hand, have to do with *means*: They fix the best, although not the sole means of fulfilling the Gospel precept and attaining the great object placed before us by God. In a parallel way, we say that air travel is the swiftest, but not the only, means of reaching a destination. Because there are a variety of suitable means for reaching the prescribed goal of life, God does not bind us all strictly to use those particular means contained in the counsels; it is sufficient that we use any suitable means—the important thing being that we all reach the end, which is love. Likewise, as observed above, there are circumstances and duties in life that make it impossible to follow the counsels; but this does not exempt anyone from observing the Gospel *law* nor from seeking the proper end of the Christian life.

In practice, therefore, we must, when discussing the obligation of the Gospel, disentangle the counsels from the precepts. Not to resist evil is a counsel, as is also the exhortation to turn the other cheek. To fail in their observance is not sinful; although, if one has the opportunity to observe them, such a failure is surely an imperfection (a sin, if it proceeds from contempt), because it is a refusal to live on the supernatural plane, to which all Christians are called. However, to love one's neighbor, even to love one's enemy, and to strive for the fullness and perfection of such love, is not a counsel but a precept. If it may be at times necessary to dispense ourselves from turning the other cheek (a dangerous dispensation, and one to be undertaken only with great caution), we may never dispense

(13) Rom. 13. 10.

ourselves from the duty to love; that is, from the substantial law which underlies the counsels.

3. In regard to the love of enemies, if the distinction ordinarily made by theologians were kept in mind, the difficulty of understanding it, and some of the difficulty of practicing it, would vanish. Were we to regard our enemies precisely as enemies, that is in so far as they inflict evil on us, then to love them would not be virtuous at all but rather, says St. Thomas, "a perversion, repugnant to charity, because this is to love evil in another." (14) But if we consider our enemies according to their rational nature, and especially according to their share, actual or potential, in the Redemption, then indeed must we love them; for our enemies are so far good, and only evil men can refuse to love what is good. Moreover, if the *substantial* fulfillment of the precept of love does not require that we love all our enemies individually and in a special way, since this would be impossible, nevertheless it demands that we love them in general according to our inward dispositions and that we are therefore ready to assist them should we be confronted by their need. (15) "Charity . . . requires, not merely as a perfection to which we ought to aim, *but as an essential necessity imposed by the precept*, not only that we should love our enemies in general, but also that our hearts should be prepared, if the necessity arose, to love them by name and individually." (16)

This lowest degree of love required of us for our enemies is already a great height; and yet we must not rest satisfied with it, releasing ourselves from further endeavor. Even where our enemies are concerned we must not stop with the lowest degree of charity, which is the substantial fulfillment of the precept, but must here likewise seek the perfection of love, since all degrees of love, even the most perfect, are contained in the precept. The perfection of love for our enemies consists in this that, whether or not they are in need, one loves them actually and not only according to an interior disposition of

---

(14) *Summa Theol.*, II II, 25, 8, c.
(15) *Ibid.*
(16) Jacques Maritain, *The Things That Are Not Caesar's*, p. 89. (New York: Scribners, 1930.)

heart. "When a neighbor is loved on account of God, then the more God is loved, the more will the neighbor also be loved, *notwithstanding the fact that he may be an enemy.* So also one who greatly loves a friend will at the same time love the friend's children, even if these should regard him with hostility." (17)

Well indeed may the Holy Father cry out, in the very midst of war, when men are bent on each other's destruction (and his words will serve to conclude and summarize this chapter), Jesus "has taught us not only to have love for those of a different nation and a different race, but to love even our enemies. While Our Heart overflows with the sweetness of the Apostle's teaching We chant with him the length, the width, the height, the depth of the charity of Christ, which neither diversity of race or culture, neither the wasteless tracts of ocean, nor wars, be their cause just or unjust, can ever weaken or destroy." (18)

---

(17) *Summa Theol.*, II II, 25, 8, c.
(18) Pius XII, Encyclical on the Mystical Body (*Mystici Corporis*).

VIII

A PEOPLE ACCEPTABLE [1]

1. One question leads to another. Now that we have established that peace, charity, and the Beatitudes are bound up with holiness, it is inevitable to ask, next, if God really asks or demands holiness of men, all men, men living in the world as well as those living in the cloister. Is holiness part of human life as God desires and designs it? What obligation has a Christian to pursue holiness? Is Christian perfection—to put the matter into terms that we have thus far been using—a precept or a counsel?

Clearly this question, or rather the answer to it, is of decisive importance and the completion of the doctrine contained in the preceding chapters. In fact, the whole force, the compulsion, behind Christ's doctrine on peace depends on this answer. If the pursuit of perfection is of counsel only, then it is clearly for the few, for select and generous souls, for those with an altogether special call from God. It will not be for men in the world; and such men are then doing exactly as they should when they leave the business of holiness exclusively to monks and nuns. Further, if perfection is of counsel only, there can scarcely be any hope that Christ's peace will ever reign in society; then the skeptics and fatalists are right—war is inevitable. Men being what they are, it is too much to hope that the mass of them will freely adopt such a lofty ideal when even the all-holy God does not expect it and seems to acquiese in the common opinion of men that perfection and holiness are impossible to them.

True, perfection, although it were only a counsel, is not for that reason to be neglected or disdained; nevertheless a counsel does not have that urgency that characterizes precepts. If it is of counsel only, then the ideal of the full Christian life and Christian society will always remain—and *must* always remain

(1) Tit. 2, 14.

—just that: an ideal, sublime and inspiring, but impracticable for the majority of men and therefore unrealizable in concrete reality.

If on the other hand the obligation to seek perfection is of precept, then we are bound as a matter of duty to translate this ideal into reality, to bring holiness into politics, economics, and international affairs. In this case, sanctity would be a normal part of human life and society as envisaged by their Creator. It would be a practicable ideal; more than that, it would be expected. It would not be a vague and delusive dream but a ground plan for social reconstruction.

Only holiness can save the world; only holiness can bring peace to human hearts and to nations. But what sanctions can be called upon to compel men to strive for it? What will constrain them at length to embrace that in which alone is to be found their salvation, temporal as well as spiritual?

2. *Perfection is a precept.* The impression, alas so widespread, that it is of counsel only, is a most mischievous error, invented surely by the father of lies, to keep us all in thralldom to himself and his kingdom of hate. Often tricked out with the appearance of theological correctness by the semi-ignorant (a little knowledge is a dangerous thing indeed), this error would release the vast majority of men from a duty that has been imposed by God upon all. It would condemn them to a life of spiritual mediocrity, to the necessity of dragging out all their days wearily on the very brink of the dread abyss of sin, with no hope of ever getting away from the immediate danger of falling and being destroyed; it would reduce all spiritual effort to a perpetual struggle, not to rise higher in the scale of holiness, but to overcome the very grossest forms of evil—a struggle, as Newman remarks, often disgraced by defeat. It would deprive men of the hope of holiness, and with it the hope of happiness, joy, peace—yes, even of salvation. It would leave the world completely to the devil by almost forbidding to good men all high endeavor and noble aspiration. It would take from human life its true purpose, fixed by God Himself. It would prevent men forever from making the first step towards that sanctity which is expected of all and that

happiness intended for all; for happiness is in holiness and the first step towards holiness is to have the desire for it.

It is not possible here to multiply proofs of this teaching. (1a) Nor is there really any need to do so. We have already shown, in the preceding chapter, that all men are obliged to seek the highest degree of love, love without measure, the totality of love. Now this love is identical with perfection and supernatural holiness. "The perfection of the Christian life, in itself and essentially, consists in love: primarily in the love of God, secondarily in the love of neighbor, concerning which are given *the principal precepts.*" (2)

Therefore, whatever is true of love is true also of perfection. And since love is not a counsel, but a commandment, and even the principal commandment, you see the central place that must be given in the Christian life to the pursuit of perfection. Why is this surprising? Was it not God's plan from the beginning? "He chose us . . . before the foundation of the world, that *we should be holy and without blemish in His sight in love.*" (3)

To say that we are bound to seek perfection, let it be noted, does not mean that we must attain to this goal all at once, here and now, for this would in truth be impossible. It means rather that we must direct our efforts towards perfection as towards our final goal, and that every day until death we ought to grow in the love of God and neighbor. In taking a trip, the last place that we reach is our destination; but we would not reach it at all did we not, from the first, desire and intend it. No Christian may excuse himself from seeking the higher degrees of divine love; if he is incapable of realizing them at once, he must at any rate aspire to them and exercise great diligence in working for them. "The end of the commandment is charity." (4)

It sometimes happens that Catholic pacifists are sneered at as "perfectionists." Their hopes are mere dreams, it is said,

---

(1a) I have treated this subject more fully in the pamphlet, "This is the Will of God" (Our Sunday Visitor Press, Huntington, Ind.).
(2) St. Thomas, *Summa Theol.*, II II, 184, 3, c.
(3) Eph. 1, 4.
(4) I Tim. 1, 5.

and their efforts are futile; they expect and demand perfection, and perfection is impossible. You see now that sneers directed at the "perfectionist" are in the end aimed at Him who said, "You therefore are to be perfect even as your heavenly Father is perfect." (5)

Holiness, therefore, is not a desirable but optional goal: it is God's law. If men had obeyed this law, they would now have the peace which they desire. Because they have disobeyed, they are now being punished. Men of our day are paying the awful penalty for treating the perfection of holiness as "a mere counsel," for using the divine law with contempt, for regarding the Sermon on the Mount only as a piece of fine rhetoric and a beautiful expression of Christ's poetic soul. "It is a fearful thing to fall into the hands of the living God." (6) The Sermon on the Mount, the law of total love, the precept of perfection and the obligation to seek for holiness —these are not mere poetry but God's eternal legislation for the human race. You may see in the social, economic and political ruin of the world today what the anger of the All-Just God will do when His decrees are neglected and despised.

3. Even the counsels of the Gospel, although they do not have the same obligation as precepts, are not to be dismissed as unimportant or irrelevant to ordinary life. Because they are not in all cases a strict duty, we must not fall into the too common error of treating them with indifference or contempt. They are *explicit manifestations of the divine will* and may therefore *never* be regarded slightingly by *anyone*. St. Francis de Sales says that one who despises the counsels is guilty of grave sin. "Now I say . . . that it is not a sin not to practice the counsels. No, in truth, Theotimus: for it is the very difference between commandments and counsels, that the commandment obliges us under pain of sin, and the counsel only invites us without pain of sin. Yet I distinctly say that to contemn the aiming after Christian perfection is a great sin, and it is still greater to contemn the invitation by which our Savior calls us to it; but it is an insupportable impiety to contemn the counsels and means

(5) St. Matt. 5, 48.
(6) Heb. 10, 31.

which our Savior points out for the attainment of it. It were a heresy to say that our Savior had not given us good counsel, and blasphemy to say to God: Depart from us, we desire not the knowledge of Thy ways: (7) but it is a horrible irreverence against Him who with so much love and sweetness invites us to perfection, to say: I will not be holy or perfect, nor have any larger portion of Thy benevolence, nor follow the counsels which Thou givest me to make progress in perfection." (8)

Those who are not strictly obliged by the counsels, or who are placed in circumstances where it is not possible to observe them fully or at all, may nevertheless find in them a guide to the divine will and therefore a general indication at least of the line that human conduct must take if it is to conform to God's providential plan. "If it is the essence of a counsel not to require strict obedience, and if, therefore, the inferior may have valid reasons for not executing materially whatever the superior more or less instantly suggests to or requires from him, there is, nevertheless, even so, a *providential direction in the action of the superior which an intelligent obedience can distinguish and retain.*" (9)

All Christians, whether lay or religious, should search out this "providential direction" in the counsels in relation to themselves and their own circumstances. Thus, ultimately, even the counsels should influence the everyday activity of Christians and the spirit of the counsels should direct, not only the lives of religious, but also what are called the secular affairs of all men. Indeed if God's will were taken as guide for human life, there would be no such thing as secular affairs divorced from the influence of religion.

To put the matter differently: All are bound to observe the spirit of the counsels and to practice the interior virtues of which the counsels are simply the external form and expression. Although a man in the world, because of his personal needs and his family obligations, cannot take a vow of poverty,

(7) Job 21, 14.

(8) *Treatise on the Love of God*, Bk. VIII, Chap. 8. (Westminster, Md., The Newman Bookshop, 1942).

(9) Jacques Maritain. *The Things That Are Not Caesar's*, p. 26. Italics ours.

he must none the less exercise the virtue of poverty and cultivate a spirit of detachment from the goods of the world; for these are required of all. If it is not his vocation to make a vow of chastity, it is nevertheless his duty to practice chastity according to his state in life, whether married or unmarried. If he has not made a vow that binds him to obey a religious superior, he must, simply as a Christian, exercise obedience towards his lawful superiors and all the divine decrees in his regard.

Thus—allowances being made for the varying obligations of diverse states in life—lay Christians as well as monks must practice poverty, chastity, and obedience. Similarly (to apply these principles to the present subject) all must practice meekness and humility; for these are the virtues which underlie the counsel of non-resistance to evil. Even when the Christian is bound by duty to resist evil, as may sometimes happen; even when it would be wrong for him to turn the other cheek, he must not for a moment, whatever the circumstances, cease from the practice of humility, meekness, and love of enemies.

If a Christian is unable to adopt, because of particular circumstances, the external form of conduct recommended in the Gospels he must never abandon the interior dispositions which are the heart of these forms. He may be unable to use the *best* means of seeking holiness, but he may never cease from striving after holiness itself and the fullness of love. He may not dispense himself from using *some adequate means* of working for the end of Christian life. He may never, even in the midst of secular affairs, deviate from the way that leads to this goal or from those virtues and dispositions which are a *necessary means* of reaching it.

Meekness, detachment, indifference to honors of the world—these, the interior dispositions which lie at the heart of the counsels—are integral parts of Christian perfection and are enjoined upon us all by Almighty God. They are necessary, in the first place, to prepare the soul for the reception of grace and charity; they dredge from it the impurities that would prevent these divine gifts from flowing into the soul. They are, further, and for the same reason, necessary for obtaining and increasing divine love. They are, finally, the inevitable expression of the soul's love for God: "This is love, that we walk according to His commandments." (10) In a word, these dispositions and virtues center around the great law of love. They are intended to make possible and to facilitate the operation of that law. That is why they are necessary: not because of themselves, but because of their connection with the law of love. The kingdom of God in a soul is like a beautiful city raised in a wilderness. To build such a city, there must first be pioneers to clear the way, workers to dredge streams, reclaim land, dig and build foundations; others to construct, to conserve, to repair, to guard and defend the city. So also divine love, to establish itself in a soul, requires analogous preparation and care; and this is the office of the virtues and dispositions which are fostered by the counsels.

Accordingly, ordinary Christians—all Christians in fact—have an obligation to follow the counsels, so far as this is possible, and at least according to their spirit. This obligation is serious and comes with the Gospel itself; it is an obligation of love. To say that turning the other cheek to an "enemy" (a Christian has no enemies!) is a counsel means simply that failure to do so in a particular case is not a sin and cannot therefore prevent one from entering heaven. It does not mean, however, that he is exempt from the law of love or even from the lesser virtue of meekness. Let it be observed also that if a Christian goes beyond cases and all his life neglects the counsels, he will in the end fail to fulfill the essential precept of Christian life or to reach his proper goal. If a man will not travel by air, he can still reach his destination by other means; but what if he refuses all other means of transportation also?

4. To this it must be added that the spirit of the counsels, to which all are bound, is by far the more important part of them. This is true even of religious, who are bound to observe the letter also. The spirit is the core, the kernel, the animating force. Without detachment from the goods of the world, poverty is no more meritorious than good health. Without detachment from carnal desires, external chastity has no moral

(10) II St. John 1, 6.

or supernatural value and is not incompatible with grave sin. Without detachment from one's own will, obedience is rather hypocrisy than virtue. If a religious takes the vow of poverty but lacks its spirit, having a habitual affection to the vanities and riches of the world, his conduct will be more likely to bring down the divine anger than divine grace. So with the other counsels. Laymen, therefore, should not say that, since they have not taken religious vows, they are bound *only* by the spirit of the counsels, as though this were the lesser thing. The humility that accepts injury from others, the meekness that accepts it with a calm and gentle spirit, the love that embraces those who cause the injury—this is the very substance and marrow of God's eternal law.

For all these reasons, if a Christian, taking advantage of the fact that he may protect himself without fault, actually does defend his rights or his person against injury *on account of the common good* (this is the only reason which St. Augustine and St. Thomas assign as valid for such an exemption) (11), he should enter into his defense, not fiercely or angrily or in a spirit of vindictiveness, but gently and from a motive of supernatural love, in the manner in which fervent religious go into the choir to chant *Lauds.*

Similarly, should a nation believe itself compelled to go to war, for the sake of justice and the common good, at the same time setting aside the Gospel counsel that would have us suffer evil, its citizens and soldiers must nevertheless conduct themselves in a manner compatible with the Gospel notions of holiness and love. They are not to act out of hatred or a desire for vengeance, for in this case they would destroy the charity and the zeal for justice which (it is assumed in the very nature of a just war) are inspiring their military expedition.

Is this the way in which modern nations go to war? Americans (to keep our eyes on ourselves) went into World War II with revenge on their lips and, it is to be feared, in their hearts as well. "Remember Pearl Harbor!" they cried, and the chorus was taken up all over the nation. The whole spirit of the war with Japan has been one of revenge, the Japanese people being

(11) *Summa Theol.*, II II, 40, 1, ad 2.

popularly represented as cruel, subhuman monsters who must be slain as a matter of elementary decency. (11a) Nor was this sentiment confined to the ignorant and illiterate; high government officials, army and navy officers were just as guilty.

The government itself, in February, 1944, released a series of atrocity stories describing in horrid detail the treatment to which American prisoners had been subjected by the Japanese. These stories had been withheld from publication many months for reasons not explained; they were released (by a remarkable coincidence) at the very time that the Fourth War Loan was being launched and the President was asking for the conscription of women in his message to Congress. The nation rose up and demanded revenge ("Revenge! The Nation Demands It"—was a headline in the New York Times). We were treated to the spectacle of United States Senators shouting like young bullies in an alley fight and boasting of a determination to "get even." With this fine motive (but is it the Gospel motive?) the sales of war bonds increased of course; and, more important still, the American people were put in the mood to set aside all humanity and allow any methods whatsoever in a war that now became "a war without quarter." Following the stories of the above mentioned atrocities, a writer in the New York Times commented as follows (12):

"Moreover, *there will be less moral repugnance than ever before* against the use of certain methods of warfare that we have hitherto refrained from using. Gas has frequently been suggested as a possible weapon in the Pacific; those who favor it *justify it morally on the ground that China claims Japan has used it against her.*

"Gas is generally greatly overrated by the lay mind as an effective military tactic; just as the lay mind wrongly ascribes to it alone a peculiar moral malignancy, *which, how-*

(11a) It is of course readily forgotten (it should be very sobering to remember) that the barbarism of the Japanese, as reported in the press, is due in no small measure to the failure of Christian peoples to work seriously for the conversion of Japan. Had the people of Western nations been as zealous to carry the cross to Japan as they now are to bring the sword there, it would not now be thought necessary to carry the sword.

(12) Sunday, Jan. 30, 1944. Section 4. Italics ours.

ever, should also properly be shared by high explosives, tanks, etc. But if gas should be found militarily useful by our commanders in the Pacific, there would probably be *far less compunction about its use, on the part of the American public today, than there was ten days ago.*

"In other words, the Pacific War is becoming more and more—to put it bluntly—a 'no-quarter' war, *in which no holds will be barred.* On many of the fighting fronts it was already a 'no-quarter' war; but now, if new devices and new methods, such as gas, are not used, it will *not be primarily because of the compunctions of public opinion,* but because the enemy in Europe—Germany—*might retaliate,* or because of the lack of military effectiveness of the new devices."

There is the candid confession of the most complete paganism and lack of moral principle; this is the law of reprisal, not that of love. May a people animated by such sentiments of revenge claim to represent and fight for justice and Christian civilization?

Though soldiers and generals are not bound *by the letter* of the counsels, they must conduct their wars in the spirit of the counsels. (How this is to be done is their problem.) In any event their exemption from the letter of the counsels is not a permission to indulge in revenge and hatred. How, then, can Allied leaders commit every enormity that is deplored in "the enemy," condemning such methods as barbarous and inhuman in the enemy and nevertheless adopting them at the same time with the explanation that "they did it first"? There has been scarcely any measure employed by the totalitarian countries, no matter how monstrous, which has not been taken up, and without much hesitation or scruple, by the "Christian democracies." Perhaps the Germans were the first to destroy civilian populations and whole cities; but when the Allies had once got started, they really showed how destruction should be done and they prided themselves on their thoroughness. The defense was always the same: they did it, therefore we must do it. The writer of the above excerpt calls this a principle of morality; it is rather a principle of immorality.

Surely this is to make a mockery out of the Gospel, both

counsel and precept. Contrast such attitudes and methods with the strategy recommended by the Scriptures for overcoming our enemies: "If thy enemy is hungry, give him food; if he is thirsty, give him drink; for by so doing thou wilt heap coals of fire upon his head." (13)

---

(13) Rom. 12, 20.

IX
EVANGELIC PACIFISM

1. It is time to recapitulate, bring together, and apply the various principles that have been described in these pages. Having before us, clearly and simultaneously, these several doctrines concerning the precept of charity, the duty to seek perfection, and the force of the counsels, it is possible now to point them towards practice and to discover how far Catholics may become pacifists—that is, how far they may, or should, refuse to participate in any activities that contribute to war. And the conclusion that emerges from this consideration is that war is opposed, on the one hand, to the counsels of the Gospel, but also, on the other, *to the substance and perfection of its central and essential law, that of evangelic love.* Hence war—not war *as such,* but war as it actually exists today—stands condemned by the Gospel.

First in regard to the counsels. To settle international problems by war means that the evangelic counsels are simply put to one side. Meekness, humility, turning the other cheek, and the returning of good for evil are officially ruled out of international relations. Differences among nations are then to be settled on the basis of natural law alone. That is to say, natural law would be the highest norm and ideal acknowledged even by moral and religious men. However, in practice, as experience amply demonstrates, it would be natural law crudely interpreted by the *lex talionis,* the law of retaliation, which was indeed the condition of things before the coming of Jesus. In truth, the *lex talionis* is the only code acknowledged, even in theory, by the world today—although the actual conduct of public affairs seems often to follow another, a much grosser law, that of the jungle. Perhaps this *need* not be the case (1),

(1) Theoretically, discarding the counsels would still leave, beside the law of nature, the precept of supernatural charity, intact and binding. In practice, however, as will be noted at once (the reasons have been already given in the previous chapter) supernatural charity is likely to take flight from human affairs with the evangelic counsels.

but that it is in fact the case is quite certain. Yet once and for all the *lex talionis* was set aside by Jesus: "You have heard that *it hath been said*: An eye for an eye, and a tooth for a tooth. *But I say to you* not to resist evil. . . ." (Matt. 5, 39.)

It should be noticed here, contrary to a rather frequent misunderstanding, that the *lex talionis* was not a law permitting revenge. It came from God (Exodus 21, 23-25); therefore it was holy within the limits and in the sense that the entire Old Law was holy. It did not sanction revenge or reprisals. Even in Old Testament times, revenge was claimed by God as a divine prerogative: "Revenge is mine, and I will repay in due time." (Deut. 32, 35). The *lex talionis* was a law allowing just compensation for injuries. It was primitive, but it was well suited to the condition of the half-civilized people for whom it was intended; in fact it was less primitive than the accepted practice of our "enlightened" age. It was the law of nature, sanctioned, made definite, applied. (2) Whatever its merits, however, it was replaced by Jesus, *"But I say to you. . . ."*

Perhaps it is true, as some maintain, that States may disregard the counsels. From this it would follow that all international relations, almost as a matter of duty, are to be removed from the influence of the lofty ideals of the Gospel. Not only would States be permitted to ignore the counsels *de facto* (and they really need no encouragement in this direction); they would also be enjoined to do so *de iure*. They might conceivably arrive at a more refined conception of natural law than that of the old Testament. Actually, however, no such conception exists outside of Christian thought: only Christianity preserves even human things. Add the further fact that men do not live in a state of pure nature, but in a state of fallen and corrupted nature: there is that in them which prevents them from fully realizing even a natural ideal without the assistance of grace; that is, without living a supernatural life, for grace is powerless unless men correspond with it and they correspond

(2) Thus, according to St. Thomas, the New Law did not really change or contradict the Mosaic code in this matter: it simply decreed directly and completely what God had desired from the beginning. *Summa Theol.*, I II, 107, 2 ad 2.

with it only by supernatural living. In other words, in the future, as in the past, the purely natural ideal at best will be impotent in the long run to raise and maintain mankind above the level of the beasts. (3) Not a very happy prospect for the human race!

It is therefore impossible to concede to the State a plenary dispensation from the counsels. Against such a concession stand the inadmissible conclusions just mentioned, the rejection by Jesus of the *lex talionis,* and in our day the voice of Peter, which interprets the Gospel teaching for each age, recalling the nations, not merely to the law of nature, but to the more exalted law of the Gospel. "He who would have the star of peace shine out and stand over human society should cooperate toward the setting up of a State conception and practice founded on reasonable discipline, exalted kindliness, *and a responsible Christian spirit.* . . . Do you, crusader-volunteers of a distinguished new society, lift up the new call for moral *and Christian* rebirth, declare war on the darkness which comes from deserting God, on the coldness that comes from strife between brothers. It is a fight for the human race, which is gravely ill and must be healed in the name of *conscience ennobled by Christianity.*" (4) Whatever distinction is to be made between individuals and States in regard to the moral requirements for their respective actions, there can be no question of a complete exemption of States from the yoke of Christ.

Accordingly, it is wholly certain that nations, as little as individuals, can be excused from the spirit of the counsels and the law of love. Yet in practice to throw out the letter of the counsels with contempt, as the modern world has done, leads also to the loss of their spirit. Who despises the counsels commits grave sin, said St. Francis de Sales: here in the loss of the Christ-spirit from human affairs is the wages of this sin. Furthermore, contempt of the counsels involves also a loss of charity, which is of precept; for the two are so closely bound together that contempt and neglect of the one leads to contempt and neglect for the other. This is why we see hatred

(3) See the introduction for a more complete treatment of this point.
(4) Pope Pius XII, Christmas Broadcast, Dec. 24, 1942.

and suspicion among nations, why even in peace the world has the appearance of an armed camp, why peoples are so jealous of their own glory, so determined upon their national exaltation, so sensitive about their honor, so prone to enforce their demands by threats, so ready to make an appeal to force. The spirit of the counsels has disappeared from the earth. It is now "an eye for an eye, a tooth for a tooth"—grossly misunderstood by carnal men to justify national revenge and reprisal.

There is another point to be observed in this connection. In order to train soldiers, the State must teach them *as private individuals* to disregard the Evangelical counsels, together with all those Christian virtues that inculcate meekness, gentleness, humility, mildness. That is to say, since "nations are indeed but collections of individuals" (5), the public repudiation by the State of these specifically Christian virtues reacts on the private lives of the soldiers, their families, their communities. Meekness and gentleness are not taught in the courses of military training, although they are certainly an important part of the pattern of living given us by Jesus. On the contrary, it is pride of strength, the ambition for glory, anger, revenge, hatred, contempt for weakness, brutality, and cruelty that are released by war. Since modern armies are numbered by the millions, this is a fact of the gravest importance. Whole populations are deprived of the opportunity and the necessary incentives for the difficult task of imitating Christ. The influence of Christian virtues is removed from all civil and social life. . . . Are States within even their "natural" rights in thus exiling the spirit of Christ from the world?

2. However, war today not merely forces men to abandon the letter and spirit of the counsels (although this alone would be its sufficient condemnation), but *it is opposed also to the substance and the perfection of the Christian life,* that is, to the greatest and first of the precepts, that of love, which Christians are bound to observe.

As to the substance of the precept, it requires, as minimum, that God be loved above all creatures and that our neighbors, including enemies, be loved as ourselves, at least, as already

(5) Pope Benedict XV, *Pacem Dei.*

explained, in general and according to an inward disposition of the heart. Now war (always speaking of war in the concrete, as it exists now) offends against both the love of God and of neighbor. Let us examine each of these manifestations of love.

War is opposed to the love of God because *its motive*, which determines (and reveals) its final end, that to which it is ultimately subordinated, is the love for riches and the desire for earthly goods and honor. Not love for God nor zeal for God's honor, nor even zeal for justice, is its motive. Nor is it subordinated *ultimately* to God; it serves Him in no way at all. On the contrary, it involves a genuine preference for creatures over God, so that its root cause, as has been shown elsewhere, is *the idolatry of creatures*. (6) Accordingly it will stop at nothing to satisfy the greed which is its motive; and its actual conduct is therefore marked by violations of all the laws that God has laid down to govern human actions: undeniable proof that it does not satisfy even the minimum requirement, for the lowest degree of love acceptable to God is that involved in obedience to the Ten Commandments.

While there is not opportunity here to describe fully all the injustices that enter into modern war, a short digression will make clear the grossness and iniquity of war's essential motive and the incompatibility of such a motive with that of love.

Whatever war is in theory (or might be in practice, were governments and armies to observe the neat but complicated rules given by moralists), in actual reality it is the method used by great nations to implement "power politics." Its purpose is to secure and guarantee the dominance of some particular nation, or nations, by control of wealth and economic resources; also to weaken, or to keep weak, countries whose power might be a threat to the dominant powers. Instead of being a last resort, as moralists demand, it is an alternative—that is, it is the second and more powerful of the two normal means employed by governments to achieve the ends mentioned. Diplomacy is the other means, but diplomacy by itself would be weak and ineffectual: war is its reinforcement, its

(6) *The Weapons of the Spirit.*

sanction, and its alternative. Both diplomacy and war have for their aim to impose the will of one nation on the people of another. Hence the oft-quoted dictum of Clausewitz, greatest of philosophers of war, that war is a continuation of policy *by other means*. And his definition: "War is an act of violence intended to compel our opponent to do our will." (7)

Every foreign commitment made by any nation, Mr. Walter Lippman points out, (8) requires sufficient military power to defend it, together with readiness to exercise this power if there is need. War is the result of a conflict of such commitments, which are motivated by love of wealth and power, urged on by the insatiable appetite of the Industrial-Capitalistic system, and entered into through commercial enterprises and the exploits of national imperialism; else it is the conflict between those who have such commitments and those who desire to have them. So does war issue from the union of the two greatest modern social evils, economic imperialism and nationalism.

The Allied Nations, in both World Wars, while alleging ethical defense as their motive, were actually defending material gains obtained by past unjust wars, diplomatic trickery and pressure, and various other methods of exploitation, whether legalized or violent. They have fought two great wars to defend these huge, ill-gotten empires and thereby to maintain political or economic dominance, or both, over the other nations of the world—a hegemony to which they have no ethical right but only a "claim" based on economic resources, swollen national pride and the myth of racial superiority. The very possession of these empires, their monopoly of the wealth and the material resources of the world, is itself a threat to the peace of nations, an act of aggression, an occasion and cause for envy, hatred, conflict—and war. Thus while seeking to place the full blame for both World Wars on Germany, the

(7) Quoted from "*Modern War and Basic Ethics*," by John K. Ryan. (Milwaukee: Bruce & Co., 1940.)

(8) *U. S. Foreign Policy:* Shield of the Republic. (Boston: Little, Brown & Co., 1942.) Readers who do not think that the United States is imperialistic are referred to this book. Also to *How New Will the Better World Be?* by Carl L. Becker, Chapter IV. (New York: Alfred Knopf, 1944.)

Allies were themselves the chief authors of the system from which modern war has developed. Their wars have no greater moral dignity than the rivalries and raids of pirates.

Clearly, then, not love of God nor zeal for His justice, nor even the right of self-preservation, but rather love for the perishable goods of this world is the true cause of war. And this excludes the very substance and minimum of that love required of man for God. For, as St. Thomas says, "Man is placed midway between the goods of this world and those of the spirit (in which his eternal happiness is to be found): so that the more he is attached to either class of these goods, the further is he removed from the other, and vice versa. He, therefore, who is wholly attached to the things of the world, to the extent that he makes them his end, and takes from them the motives and norm (*rationes et regulas*) of his actions, is wholly cut off from spiritual goods." (9) Little wonder then that nations, having thus excluded the love of God from their actions from the beginning, do not in the conduct of their wars stop at any injustice or refrain from any horror but willingly take up every method, however cruel or unjust, that will advance their "interests."

3. That war is opposed to the love of neighbor appears with even greater clarity. Indeed, since the cause of war, in the first place, is so bound up with an unjust distribution of wealth, the defense or extension of this maldistribution by force of arms offends, not only against charity, but also against the more elementary virtue of justice. God put the goods of the material world here, not for the aggrandizement of nations greedy for power, but for all men, that they might have the material goods required for virtuous living. When great nations use their strength to despoil the world, like pirates fighting one another for loot, they make impossible from the very beginning the realization of that law by which all men are to be joined to one another in mutual love.

Furthermore, national rivalries over material goods breed hatred and mutual distrust just as surely as they bring war, and to a greater or less extent even before they bring war.

(9) *Summa Theol.*, I II, 108, 4, c.

War itself, in practice, cannot exist without hatred. The Nazis frankly preached hatred from the start of the Second World War: they recognized its necessity for total war. At first the Allies used this very fact as a propaganda weapon against the Nazis; but when their own leaders discovered, by costly experience, that men under their command were no match for enemies inflamed by a passionate enthusiasm, they changed their ways and began a hate propaganda as crude and barbarous as that of the Nazis. Catholics, knowing that there is no suspension of the law of love, even during war, protested from time to time, and pointed out that just war could and should be conducted *with love.* This was excellent theory, sufficient to satisfy the conscience of those who advocated war without accepting its reality. Of course they thought it was practical too, and pointed to the example of Joan of Arc who nursed her fallen foes and wept over them. However, the solitary example of one saint does not make such an ideal theory practicable for the mass of men who are anything but saints. Even in Joan's army, she is the only one who is recorded as having wept. In our day the actual fact is that hatred was taught deliberately and by principle, because leaders slowly came to realize that it was a military necessity. (10)

There is the further fact that the atrocities of war themselves are calculated to arouse hatred. In this country, the atrocities attributed to Germans and Japanese were skillfully used to arouse feelings of revenge against them. On the other hand, the savage bombing of cities by Allied fliers caused Ger-

(10) To show the method (and the fruit) of such propaganda, here is an article entitled, "Hate Your Enemy" taken from the bulletin board in a U. S. Army camp; it had been transcribed from an army publication: "Because they hated him [i.e., because the police hated John Dillinger], their efforts to corner the bandit were intensified. They finally killed him like a mad dog in a Chicago alley—and were happy in his death. That's the way you've got to feel about the Germans and Japanese and Italians. . . . War is a business of killing or being killed. Those enemies of ours don't fight by book. . . . An eye for an eye, says the old Mosaic law, a tooth for a tooth. The hell with that! Our enemies taught the world a savagery that most of us thought had died with Attila, the Hun. They must be paid for it. . . . We'll do better here, and in the theatres of operation, if we hate the bastards, as they deserve to be hated." To men who can think and feel like this, how contemptible, weak, and inopportune must seem the Church's untiring insistence on the virtue of love, on love, not only of one's own country, but also of enemies and of all mankind.

mans to hate the Americans and British. It also had the effect, not of destroying German morale as was hoped, but of stiffening it, for it convinced even Germans not in sympathy with the Nazi philosophy that their side must win or they themselves face complete destruction. (11)

Civilians also are inflamed by hatred of the enemy. Indeed, among these, including women and children, it is common to hear the most shocking expressions of contempt, hatred, and revenge. Pictures of the "enemy," dead or wounded or captured, with suitable captions, provide sadistic entertainment for the folks at home. Moving pictures, seeking to satisfy the same appetites, spare nothing of their portrayal of the gruesome details of battle, although regularly careful to show only the "enemy" dead. Heroes are feted at home because of the number of "enemies" they have killed. Pilots are decorated for planes they have shot down; and they themselves vie with one another to raise their "scores"—as though this were a game, not a fearful matter of life and death, of salvation or damnation for countless souls. Worst of all, children are subjected to "patriotic" propaganda and brought to accept the same code—to hate enemies, to accept killing as a matter of course, to regard war as a game of glory and honor, and to cheer all its horrors as long as these exalt the national cause. Thus they are trained from the cradle to acquiesce in war and to glory in it—excellent conditioning for the next war. It is indeed in this way that war becomes a self-perpetuating evil. However, the point here is that it presupposes hatred, spreads hatred, increases hatred. It is opposed to the minimum requirements of Christianity and the law of love. It is a work of the devil and as such is utterly opposed to Christ. "Satan is hatred and Christ is love."

4. Finally, war is opposed to the perfection of the Christian

(11) "The strengthening of German morale through this fear complex has been heightened by the hatred caused by American and British air raids on Germany. Reports were current in Baden-Baden, where I was interned, that the throats of many American and British pilots who were shot down or who bailed out over Hamburg literally were cut by the civilians who captured them before police or soldiers could formally imprison them." Taylor Henry, former bureau chief of Associated Press at Vichy, France (Dispatch of March 16, 1944).

life. In addition to the reasons just now given, which, if they are opposed to the substance of charity, are *a fortiori* opposed to its perfection, let it be added that the methods of modern warfare (to put the matter quite mildly) are scarcely an apt means for the pursuit of Christian perfection. The reader may recall here what has already been said concerning these methods in preceding chapters and the difficulty of reconciling them with the Christian ideal of living. Methods that are used without regard even for moral law can scarcely be considered suitable and proportioned means for helping men to advance in holiness and increase in divine love. They are opposed to the fullness of the Christian life. Because all men are obliged to the summits of perfection, and this by the law of God, they certainly may, and must, refuse to perform any actions that make the fulfillment of that law impossible. "If it be just in the sight of God to hear you rather than God, judge ye!" (12)

The supreme duty of a Christian is the imitation of Christ. His supreme privilege, as also his perfection, is resemblance to Christ. Those who are "sons of God" are recognizable as such in the degree of their likeness to Him who is their brother and the "first-born among many brethren." (13) Therefore, any condition in society that hinders the imitation of Christ stands condemned by His law. Any arrangement which prevents men from taking up this great spiritual undertaking, which is expected of all, has no validity, no force, no sanction in eternal law. Any situation created by men, together with whatever circumstances result from their actions, which are opposed to the fullness of Christian life, are iniquitous; and it is therefore a duty to change or modify them until they subserve the divine plan. Human society and secular governments, for all their preoccupation with terrestrial ends, have the duty to assist their members and subjects in obtaining their final spiritual end and beatitude. (14)

---

(12) Acts 4, 19.

(13) St. John 1, 12; Rom. 8, 29.

(14) "Hence civil society . . . should have at heart also the interests of its individual members and that in such manner as not to hinder, but in every way to render as easy as possible the possession of that highest and unchangeable good for which all should strive."—Pope Leo XIII, *Immortale Dei*.

The soldier's life has ever been one fraught with moral dangers; and his character has ever been associated with great vices. Modern warfare has not changed this condition, but has rather made it worse. When one of God's commandments is made light of, there is a tendency to disregard them all, the reason being that all sins have a common source and root in the desire for bodily goods. (15) Thus war becomes a time of wholesale sexual immorality. In our day, millions of conscripts —instead of the thousands of volunteers who formerly made up the various national armies—are compelled to take up lives of *enforced celibacy,* for which they have no vocation and no previous moral training; they are then forced to live in an atmosphere little conducive to purity. The results are what you would expect them to be: wholesale sin, winked at—and abetted—by "Christian" governments. These governments concern themselves only to show soldiers how to avoid venereal infection—meanwhile benevolently supplying the means for onanism, a crime against nature, which our age so peculiarly takes to its affections. That numberless souls are lost is of no importance to the State. (16)

But of course it is the fifth commandment that is most violated in time of war. From its violation, indeed, the others follow, for the fifth commandment, as Father Stratmann notes (17), both logically and ethically ranks above the sixth; so that contempt for the former is certain to lead to contempt for the latter. War in our day has reached the proportions of mass slaughter; so that the fearfulness of taking human life is simply no longer felt. Even civilians are killed, not by way of unintended result, but in large numbers, deliberately, as a means of breaking the "enemy's" morale. And it is this duty to kill—indiscriminately, and with any method that a diaboli-

---

(15) *Summa Theol.,* I II, 84, 1.

(16) This sexual laxity also infects civilian life, as witness the moral deterioration of public entertainments in war time, increase of juvenile delinquency (during the Second World War, especially among girls, and on sex charges), and the frightful moral aftermath of war.

(17) *Peace and the Clergy,* p. 72. (New York: Sheed and Ward, 1936.) St. Thomas also shows that the sequence of the commandments is not haphazard or the result of chance, but rather in accord with the divine plan of order. See *Summa Theol.,* I II, 100, 6.

cally inspired science can provide—which is the ultimate dilemma for a sincere and thoughtful Christian and makes the duties of a soldier, at least as understood today, incompatible with the Christian life.

It is not that a Christian can doubt the obligation of serving his country, even to the giving up of life for it. The more faithful he is to Christ's teaching, the more perfectly will he realize this. "In this we have come to know His love, that He laid down His life for us; and we likewise ought to lay down our life for the brethren." (18) What he doubts, and denies, is the duty of hating, the duty of killing: of killing his brothers in Christ; of killing indiscriminately, without distinction between guilty and not-guilty, combatant and non-combatant; of killing with whatever barbarous and unjust weapons are given to him. If he is sure that patriotism is a virtue, and that charity, going beyond the demands of justice, binds him to love his brethren, he also knows that all men are his brethren and that he, therefore, is bound to love them all. He understands that there are higher ways of serving one's country (19) and that at any rate no duty is sufficient, in the eyes of God, to permit acts of injustice or to warrant the injury of his own soul by even the smallest intentional sin.

Even the State's right to take life is limited to those who have committed some crime. The State is itself guilty of crime if it takes the lives of innocent persons. Modern warfare, however, makes no distinction or effort to discriminate between guilty and innocent. The State forces all to participate in its wars, just or unjust, either directly by military service or indirectly by working in the war industries; and warfare demands that all of these, workers and conscripts, be killed without regard for their personal guilt.

A thoughtful and sincere Christian inevitably balks at this. Moreover, in regard also to the guilty, although the State—judging the matter on the ethical plane—has the right to take their lives by way of punishment, the true Christian, concerned above all else for souls, is loath even to take the lives of sin-

(18) I St. John 3, 14.
(19) See Chapter X, towards the end.

ners and to make himself responsible for hurrying prematurely into eternity men who are not prepared and who, except for this sudden and unprovided death, deliberately inflicted, might have more time and further opportunities to repent and change their ways. The modern State, of course, cares nothing for souls—as little for those of its own subjects as for those of its enemies. That is the reason why it can wage war without scruple. The desire of the Christian is that of St. Francis among the Mohammedans: to convert rather than to kill.

5. We cannot leave this subject without noticing the light that the principles thus far set down throw on the problem of participation in war. In our day, a growing number of men, seeing the difficulty of reconciling war with the standards of morality, and much more with the demand of the Gospel, have, by registering as Conscientious Objectors, refused to take part in war; and their claim has been allowed even by governments. The Second World War, moreover, brought to attention a group of Catholic Conscientious Objectors. Formerly Catholics, while opposing war on principle, were rather easily led by nationalistic propaganda to accept the fact of war, because of their belief in the principle of just war and their confidence in the moral integrity of their leaders. But in our time many Catholics have become so opposed to war, so little credulous of its pretenses, that they have refused to participate in it at all, whatever might be the cost to them in persecution and humiliation.

However, the claim of Catholics to the right of Conscientious Objection has sometimes been denied by their coreligionists, who see only the citizen's duty to obey lawful superiors and to defend his country. (20) Of course no one can deny that a Catholic may refuse to participate in an unjust war. Indeed, this is not only a right but is also a duty. But some Catholic Conscientious Objectors have advanced a further claim. While convinced that the Second World War is unjust, their specific

(20) Alas, that they do not see the incongruity of American Christians killing German Christians, and *vice versa*, as *a matter of Christian duty!* Or the pity and tragedy of Anglo-American Churchmen defending Allied bombing raids as being in accord with Christian principles, while their French and Belgian brethren beg for mercy in the name of Christianity!

grounds for refusing to be inducted into the armed forces is rather that war is opposed to the spirit and teaching of the Gospels, the example of Christ, and the fullness of Christian life. At times their defense of this position has not been fortunate, for they have supported it only by those sayings of Christ (like, "Turn the other cheek") which have been generally understood as counsels. For this reason, the claim of such Catholic Conscientious Objectors has sometimes been disallowed, since, as we have already observed, no one may follow a counsel if it conflicts with a duty.

An entirely new light is thrown on the matter, however, once it is clearly grasped that warfare—not war as such, but actual war in the twentieth century—is opposed to the essential spirit of the counsels, to which all are certainly bound, and also the very minimum requirements of the Gospel precept of love. When Conscientious Objection is based on a precept, and that the central and essential precept of Christianity, it is on very solid ground indeed. It is then not "merely" a "counsel of perfection" to be followed only by generous souls who voluntarily and without obligation (!) give themselves up to the pursuit of holiness; it is on the contrary, the result of living in accordance with the essential duty of Christian life. This is so true that anyone who seeks to live by the Gospels and meditates on them deeply will invariably experience an unconquerable repugnance to the taking of life, especially with the cruel and indiscriminate methods of modern warfare. Such a one will be compelled by a kind of inner necessity to refuse to contribute towards war.

Since this is the case, it is not so much Conscientious Objectors as those who engage in war today that are in need of moral justification. In the circumstances of today Christians who engage in warfare are jeopardizing their souls by entering into a proximate occasion of sin. They expose themselves to the danger, almost to the certainty, of formal sin. (21) Indeed, it appears that the only thing that can save them from sin (for

(21) Formal sin is a sin deliberately and freely committed. A material sin is an action which, although sinful in itself, nevertheless does not involve guilt in a particular case because of ignorance or want of freedom.

example, bombardiers and gunners who kill civilians and defenseless men, soldiers who obey the order not to take prisoners, those who use the cruel methods of inflicting death described as "commando tactics") is ignorance, good faith, and the fact that they act out of blind obedience. Therefore circumstances warrant, if they do not compel, a refusal on the part of Christians to bear arms, both that they may save their own souls and destroy the monstrous iniquity of total war.

Does this mean that soldiers who engage in war are guilty of sin? No—or at least it does not mean that they are guilty of formal sin. Nevertheless, they are often guilty of material sin, either directly or by cooperation; that is, they perform actions which, in themselves are really sinful, although in particular cases the soldiers are not aware of this. What saves them from formal sin is ignorance or an erroneous conception of the duties of obedience; or else, on the other hand, a genuinely heroic virtue, retained in spite of adverse circumstances.

The spirit of super-patriotism exalts the heroism of soldiers by attaching to their death *in all cases* the merit of martyrdom and promising them, as a certainty, a place in the kingdom of heaven. In this matter the fanaticism of the Japanese whose religious beliefs, it is alleged, lead them to guarantee beatitude in the next life to all, without distinction, who die in the service of their country, scarcely exceeds the enthusiasm of our own people whose zeal for the national cause leads them to make an almost identical promise. In fact, a soldier must enter into heaven on exactly the same terms that obtain for everyone else. Only the holy shall see God. If a soldier has otherwise lived a holy and truly supernatural life, if his service to his country has been an act of obedience and has not caused him to be guilty of formal sin, then he will save his soul. But if he has committed (formally) any of the crimes that are part and parcel of modern war; if, as he goes into battle, he has hatred or revenge in his heart or blasphemy on his lips—as so often happens; if vile talk, sinful amusements, sexual immorality have been his means of keeping up "morale"; if his inspiration, as he goes to his death, is the photograph of a nude or semi-nude actress or of some other harlot—then the chances for his soul's salvation are very small indeed, though his death may be ever so heroic and his courage is praised in all the religious press. The most damning of all the indictments against modern war is that, rather than helping men to their eternal salvation, as all legitimate vocations should do, it exposes them to the gravest spiritual dangers and imposes on them a manner of life better calculated to bring about moral perversion than sanctity. The soldier must also cry out, with the rest of men—and his spiritual peril makes his cry all the more poignant—

Quid sum miser tunc dicturus?
Quem patronum rogaturus
Cum vix justus sit securus? (22)

The very minimum of Christianity requires that a man should accept every evil—loss of wealth, of honor, even of life—rather than commit willingly so much as one mortal sin. A perfect Christian would suffer death rather than commit a deliberate venial sin. (23) You see here how the Gospel makes war impossible. As the Church, without explicitly condemning slavery nevertheless undermined it as an economic institution through her basic law of love, which made slavery unprofitable by demanding respect for the rights of slaves and love for their persons; so also, without condemning war as *intrinsically* evil, she nevertheless makes war impossible in practice, by outlawing, again by her laws, especially that of love, the methods necessary to make warfare thorough and successful from a military point of view.

---

(22) "What shall a wretch like me find to say in my defense? Whom shall I be able to call upon as my advocate [at the Judgment], when even a saint is hardly acceptable?"—From the *Dies Irae*, sung in Requiem Masses.

(23) According to St. Ignatius Loyola, this is the second degree humility. There is also a higher degree.

X

GRACE AND SIN

1. As soon as we begin to speak of the Christian ideal of life and society as though it could be actually realized, there are protests from "practical men" of, "Impossible! Utopian! Such a wonderful state of things is not for this world." Genuine and permanent peace, then, in this estimation, is also impossible; war is inevitable: as long as human nature is what it is there will be war; and such like.

You can easily see the results of these views. They lead to an acquiescence in evil, a refusal to seek out and destroy its causes, continuous dissensions in society resulting from this refusal, a fatalistic acceptance in our day of mechanized and total war, together with the slavery that it lays upon the poor and the far-reaching damage that it brings about in the moral and spiritual lives of all. All this is supposed to be "inevitable." The basis for this gloomy and even hopeless view is the weakness in human nature and its tendency to evil; nothing better is to be expected, we are told, of weak and imperfect men.

So it is said; and not only by pagans, of whom such fatalism might be expected, but also by Christians, in whom it is nothing less than grossest cynicism. The right view of the sinfulness of human nature leads true Christians, not to despair, but to penance, to reparation, to the work of spiritual purification, to an even greater reliance on God and His grace. It is literally a dark pagan fatalism that causes men to regard evil as inevitable and to surrender to it without battle.

No doubt it is true that the infection of sin enters deeply into human nature and all its activities. St. Paul goes so far as to say of our nature, before it is purified and regenerated by divine grace, "I know that in me, that is, in my flesh, *no good dwells.*" (1) Elsewhere he tells us that sin *abounds* (2) and

(1) Rom 7, 18. The word "flesh" here means fallen human nature, human nature stained by the effects of original sin.
(2) Rom. 5, 20.

in the same letter (Chap. 1) he paints a fearful picture of the degradation to which mankind had fallen when left to itself without divine grace.

It is certain, therefore, that *had not human nature been redeemed and regenerated,* mankind would be doomed to perpetual war and to a miserable servitude to all the blackest passions. Yet Christ *did* come, He did merit the grace to redeem and regenerate mankind. Through Him men are (or may be) *reborn,* to become *new creatures.* (3) All the dark truths that St. Paul wrote down about humanity were counterpoised by what he said about the transforming power of grace. There is no minimizing the corruption of fallen nature; had we been left to the mercy of the strong evil tendencies within it, we would *all* have been damned to misery in this world and hell in the next. But the very point of Christianity is that we were *not* left to these tendencies. St. Paul, contemplating the force of evil within himself, was constrained to cry out, "Unhappy man that I am, who shall deliver me from the body of this death?" (4) It is a cry of the deepest distress; it sounds almost like a cry of despair. Yet it is not so, for in the very next breath the saint answers his own importunate question, *"The grace of God,* by Jesus Christ my Lord." (5)

God did not abandon us to the passions of fallen nature: He redeemed, renewed it, transformed it, elevated it to the divine. This He did by communicating to us His grace, a participation in the divine life, obtained for us by Jesus Christ. And if sin is powerful, grace is vastly more powerful. If sin can pull men down to everlasting death, grace can raise them up to everlasting life. If, without grace, all men would be doomed to hell, then, on the other hand, if they respond to the pull of grace, they shall have life *and peace*: "For what was impossible to the Law, in that it was weak because of the flesh, *God has made good. . . .* For the inclination of the flesh is death, but the inclination of the spirit, life *and peace.*" (6)

As sin abounded, grace does now more abound. St. Paul

(3) St. John 3, 3; II Cor. 5, 17.
(4) Rom 7, 24.
(5) Rom. 7, 25.
(6) Rom. 8, 3-6.

shows this by contrasting the effects of Adam's sin with those of Christ's obedience and death: "But not like the offense is the gift. For if by the offense of one the many died, *much more has the grace of God,* and the gift in the grace of the one man Jesus Christ, *abounded unto the many*. . . . For if by reason of one man's offense death reigned through the one man, *much more will they who receive the abundance of the grace* and of the gift of justice reign in life through the one Jesus Christ. . . . Where the offense has abounded, *grace has abounded yet more;* so that as sin has reigned unto death, *so also grace may reign* by justice unto life everlasting through Jesus Christ our Lord." (7)

Is sin to be finally triumphant? Is the prince of darkness to prevail? If you say that sin is unconquerable, that war is inevitable, then you concede the victory to the devil over Christ. Mark that both assertions come to the same thing, namely, that sin is unconquerable and war inevitable. War results from sin, from the neglect of God and His law, from man's turning his affections towards the creatures of the world; so that, if war is inevitable, it can only be because in the first place sin is inevitable.

Would any Catholic agree that sin is inevitable? Yet sin is very easy for us to commit, difficult to overcome; the world is filled with it and there seems to be no abatement of sinfulness on the part of mankind. May we for that reason lay down our arms and capitulate to evil, saying that the struggle against it is hopeless? Sin comes from the infection in our nature which the Scriptures describe as concupiscence—an infection which it is impossible wholly to root out in this world, which remains even to tempt the saints on earth, which still fills the world with its nauseous fruits two thousand years after St. Paul described them in that terrifying first chapter in his letter to the Romans. May Christ's Church, considering this fact, cease from her endless fight against worldliness and sin? May she tell her priests to be quiet and to cease from this hopeless and Utopian effort?

You know the answer to these questions. Realizing better

(7) Rom. 5, 15-17-20-21.

than all others the terrible ravages of sin—since only a spiritual gaze can appreciate even this—the Church nevertheless does not relinquish her difficult mission of fighting evil in all its manifold forms, of vindicating the rights of God no matter how widely they may be disregarded. The fierceness, the violence, the endlessness of the struggle, and the little apparent success that she obtains, do not deter her from her high calling. Look at the pronouncements of the modern Popes: conscious that the world, and even their own children, are not heeding their words, they nevertheless go on tirelessly, like the Master whose vicar they are, reproving, entreating, rebuking, in season and out of season, in all patience and doctrine. (8)

As with sin, so with war, the result of sin. Granted that the fight against it will be long and tedious—endless, if you will, since, even if we might at length succeed in bringing under control the evil inclinations of fallen nature, there would always be the liability of resurgence. Granted that war and hatred and dissension have deep roots in our fallen nature—roots which will never be destroyed wholly in this world and which with the slightest encouragement spread and grow with the wildest luxuriance. Granted that these difficulties exist, together with as many others as you can think of, nevertheless we Christians must fight untiringly to overcome them and to end the hatred and enmity which cause war. The Popes also realize the difficulty of peace, but they go on urging men to pursue it; they deplore and condemn war; they constantly repeat the conditions that lead to true peace. They are unwearied in their fight against the evils of hatred, resolute in their efforts to establish Christ's kingdom of love. And they tell their priests, all over the world, that they too must carry on the same apostolate of peace: "It is Our especial wish," wrote Pope Benedict XV to his brother Bishops all over the world, "that you should exhort your priests, as the ministers of peace, to be assiduous in urging this love of one's neighbor and even of enemies which is the essence of Christian life, and by being all things to all men and giving an example to others, wage war *everywhere on enmity and hatred,* thus doing a thing most

(8) II Tim. 4, 2.

agreeable to the loving Heart of Jesus and to him who, how ever unworthy, holds His place on earth." (9)

To wage war *on enmity and hatred*—that is the duty of Christianity; and of all Christians!

2. Nor is the struggle a hopeless one, nor must we fight without confidence of victory. The victory is not the devil's, but Christ's. Even though it does appear outwardly that Satan has finally established his dread kingdom of hate in this world, when we see all peoples engaged in a "global war" of utter destruction, the final victory, in whatever mysterious ways it may be worked out through the Providence of God, will be Christ's. "I have overcome the world," He said. (10) And the followers of Christ are to share His triumph: "Thanks be to God, who hath *given us* the victory through Our Lord Jesus Christ." (11) If evil seems at times triumphant, let us not forget that the greatest marvel of God's Providence is that He can circumvent evil and even employ it in some mysterious way for a greater ultimate good. The crime of deicide was the means of the world's salvation. That evil seems to get worse does not need to discourage us in our fight against evil. The darkest hour is said to be just before the dawn. "The night is far advanced; the day is at hand!" (12)

Each time we repeat the Lord's prayer we say the words, "Thy kingdom come!" And this kingdom is one of peace. (13) Further, as St. Thomas teaches, (14) the petitions of the Our Father are the mold into which Jesus would have us shape our desires; they fix the object of our desires, hence also of our efforts. And the first of these petitions is for the establishment of Christ's kingdom! Did the God-man delude and mislead us by exhorting us to fix all the desire of our hearts on an object which is impossible of realization? Is not this question, seriously uttered, itself a blasphemy?

If you object that the kingdom of Christ is a spiritual kingdom, a kingdom not of this world, as He Himself said, a secret

(9) *Pacem Dei.*
(10) St. John 16, 33.
(11) I Cor. 15, 57.
(12) Rom. 13, 12.
(13) Rom. 14, 7.
(14) *Summa Theol.*, II II, 83, 9, c.

and hidden world that exists only in the souls of men, then reflect on the next, the second of the petitions in the Lord's prayer, which adds to our understanding of the first: "Thy will be done *on earth* as it is in heaven." "Meditate on these things, give thyself entirely to them. . . ." (15)

It is an error and a heresy to limit Christ's kingdom to the interior world of the individual's spiritual life. We have a special feast, inaugurated in our own day, to remind us that Christ is universal king of the world. It is true, Christ's kingdom is spiritual, not of this world. But this means only that He would have the world break from its allegiance to the devil, whom He calls its prince, and be dominated instead by the law of the Spirit; He wants divine truth to govern men in all their activities, even such as are called secular, as well as in their relationships with one another. It was His aim, not only to convert us to the love of God by means of an interior life, but also to bind us to one another by love. He definitely included man's social relationships in His legislation; what is more, He made these relationships the peculiar object of His care: "A new commandment I give unto you, that you love one another." (16) In these words, so familiar as to have become trite, and nevertheless almost wholly unknown, Jesus laid down the supreme law that was henceforth to govern all human relationships, and therefore society itself.

Jesus, although recognizing that the world was under the sway of the devil, did not abandon it to the devil. He demanded that men change their allegiance and henceforth give their loyalty to Him. And the loyalty He required is a complete one: not only men's hearts, not only their interior life—though certainly this in the first place—but also their minds, their souls, their strength. All human activity, all human life, all human achievement, is to be subordinated to Him; for it is the eternal plan of the Father "in the dispensation of the fullness of times, *to re-establish all things in Christ,* that are in heaven and *on the earth,* in Him." (17)

(15) I Tim. 4, 15.
(16) St. John 13, 34.
(17) Eph. 1, 10.

Hence, although Jesus did not go into the details of sociological study or inaugurate any specific social reforms, He nevertheless promulgated the great law that was to establish society on a supernatural basis. We may add that He did as much for economics, enunciating the truth and fixing the law that was to re-establish this science also on a supernatural foundation: "Seek ye therefore first the kingdom of God and His justice, and all these things shall be added unto you." (18)

The assertion, so frequently made, that Jesus did not interfere in the social and economic problems of His day is misleading even if strictly true. If a man leaves a time-bomb in a building it is not necessary for him to stay there to see what will happen. Our Lord, although He laid down no economic or sociological principles in the scientific sense, did place in the world, in His commandment of entire love of God and love of neighbor, a force that would in due time change the whole world. "Behold *all things* are made new!" (19)

3. No doubt, there will always be differences in opinion, variations of judgment among men, even among Christian men, even among saints. The existence of such differences does not need to disturb their peace nor is it an argument that peace can never exist. Differences of opinion are in the intellect or the judgment, whereas love (and therefore also peace) is in the will or heart. AS LONG AS THERE IS A UNION OF WILLS in the choice of the final end of life, a union of desires for the great good of life, which is God, and a union of hearts in the love of God, there will be peace even in the midst of intellectual disagreements as to how these ends are to be realized. If men are at one in the choice of a final end, their differences can only be minor ones concerning the means to be employed. Such is the doctrine of St. Thomas. (20) Men living in the kingdom of God, and hungering and thirsting after justice, will have peace in their hearts and wills for they will be united in the one great matter that really counts; their differences will be only in deciding how they are best to satisfy their spiritual hunger and thirst.

---

(18) St. Matt. 6, 33.
(19) II Cor. 5, 17.
(20) *Summa Theol.*, II II, 29, 3, ad 2.

Of course the peace that is obtainable in this world, as St. Thomas also says, is imperfect, whereas perfect peace will be enjoyed in the world to come. Yet the difference between perfect and imperfect peace is one of degree, not of kind, and is similar to that between the supernatural happiness of this world and that of the next, between the life of grace and the life of glory, between seeing the things of God now "through a mirror . . . but then face to face." (21) The life of grace, lived in this world, is a kind of beginning, *quaedam inchoatio,* of the life of glory; whereas the life of glory in heaven is the culmination and fulfillment of the life of grace, the supernatural life, which we ought to live in this world. "Grace is glory in exile," Father Faber wrote, "and glory is grace at home." So that all the gifts of the Spirit—love, holiness, joy, peace—which we hope perfectly to possess in our heavenly home may be possessed here already, not perfectly it is true, but in a manner altogether real and sufficient for our requirements in this world.

Therefore, making whatever reservations need to be made, it is still true that a tranquillity of order can be realized even in this world and that the peace of Christ ought even here to bind men together. Indeed, the enjoyment of peace belongs essentially to the Christian vocation. "And may the peace of Christ reign in your hearts; unto that peace indeed you were called in one body." (22) To hold otherwise is, ultimately, not to convict those who do so believe and hope of unrealism, but to make Jesus Himself guilty of this mistake. What we are talking about is *Christ's* religion, *Christ's* kingdom, *Christ's* law, *Christ's* peace. If they cannot be realized, it is because Christ was a visionary. If they do not take account of reality, then it is to Christ, the very Incarnate Wisdom of God, that this ignorance and shallowness must be attributed. If they do not allow for the exigencies and the weakness of human nature, then it is Christ, through whom human nature was created, that we must charge with failure to understand it. But if

(21) I Cor. 13, 12.
(22). Col. 3, 15.—Note that this "calling" includes social peace—"in one body."

Christ was in truth the Son of God; if in fact all power was given to Him in heaven *and on earth*; if He is King of all nations and peoples; if He is the infinite Wisdom of God—then may we, with reliance on His knowledge of all obstacles and difficulties, and with confidence in His power to overcome them, hopefully strive for the establishment of His Kingdom of peace on earth.

XI

"HE IS OUR PEACE . . ."

1. There is none better fitted to speak of peace than the Church of Christ. She has the right, and indeed the duty, to do so by divine appointment. Already in the Old Testament the Messias was heralded by Isaias as "the Prince of Peace." When He at length came into the world, He was accompanied by a promise of peace: "And on earth, peace to men of good will." (1) Again, upon leaving the world, one of His last gifts was, "Peace be to you." (2)

If the promise of peace has nevertheless not been fulfilled, at least visibly, this fact is also in accordance with prophecy. As Christ was to bring about the rise of many, that is, their elevation to the dignity of the sons of God, together with the eternal joy and peace that this immense privilege would bring, so also was He set for the fall of many. Some, rejecting Him and His teaching, would on that account not be able to obtain the rich and precious gifts which He brought us. The coming of Christ's peace is contingent upon the acceptance of Christ.

It is instructive to notice that the punishment of those who rejected Christ was precisely this, that they were deprived of peace, that "most beautiful gift of God, the name of which, as St. Augustine says, is the sweetest word to our hearing and the best and most desirable possession." (3) Weeping over Jerusalem, Jesus said, "If thou hadst known, and that in this thy day, *the things that are to thy peace.*" Then He added words even more terrible, illustrating how neglect of grace blinds men to the extent that they no longer even know where to look for what they desire most: *"But now they are hidden from thy eyes."* (4)

If mankind, after 1900 years of having Christ's Church in its

(1) St. Luke 2, 14.
(2) St. John 20. 21.
(3) Benedict XV, *Pacem Dei*.
(4) St. Luke 19, 42.

midst, has not yet found the secret of peace, it is for the same reason; like Jerusalem, it has rejected Christ. Christ weeps over the modern world as He did over Jerusalem, and He says over us, as over that fair and faithless city, "If thou hadst known the things that are to thy peace!" Likewise, as men today look eagerly and hopelessly about for peace—everywhere but in the direction from which true peace can come—it seems that neglect of grace has reduced them, as it did the Jews, to the spiritual blindness which prevents them forever from seeing the things that are to their peace.

There is a tendency to regard those Scriptural texts which associate peace with Jesus as merely figurative or poetical, as though such expressions were but the result of a fervent love and admiration which, seeking expression, caused the sacred writers to multiply titles of honor to satisfy their enthusiasm. Even when Jesus Himself speaks of peace and promises it to His followers, His words are seldom taken literally and seriously. This is sufficiently proven by the fact that the concrete realization of His Kingdom of peace is regarded as impossible, as well as by the obstinate persistence with which even those who claim to be His followers and who employ His slogans of peace nevertheless make no practical efforts to achieve "peace by Christ Jesus" but rather place their entire confidence in the great ones of the world—statesmen, diplomats, jurists, and (most remarkable of all) generals.

The Savior's power to give peace is a reality, not a figure. We ought therefore to place clearly before ourselves the doctrinal grounds upon which rests His claim to be in very truth "the King of Peace." (5) Firm convictions in this matter will bring about two most salutary results. They will compel us to make practical peace efforts in Christ and through Christ. Secondly, they will show us why it is, and how true it is, that those who seek to be conformed to Christ must be peacemakers.

2. Christ is King of Peace in three ways: in His being; in virtue of His office; by His conduct and example.

In His being. To say that Jesus is master of peace, or that He possesses peace, or even that He is the very source of peace,

(5) Heb. 7, 2.

is an inadequate statement of the truth. In speaking of the love of God, the Scriptures do not say merely that God has love; they do not say even that God has the fullness of love. They say that God *is* love. In other words, love is His very essence; He is Himself the infinity of love; and we can therefore form no better or truer idea of what God is than by thinking of love in its most exalted condition, infinite, all-embracing, personal. Similarly, in speaking of peace, the Scriptures climax all their other numerous utterances by saying, "He *is* our peace." (6) Jesus is the very source and substance of peace, and those who desire peace may obtain it as they approach nearer and nearer to Him; just as an object gets more heat the closer it is brought to a fire.

In His divine nature—that is, as the Word of God and second Person of the Blessed Trinity—it is true to say that Jesus is our peace in the same way in which it is true to say that He is love. For peace, as we have observed, is but the activity and fruit of love. In God, who is infinitely simple and therefore without division of parts, peace and love cannot be distinct from each other or from His essence. They are—they must be—identical with His essence: He *is* love; He *is* peace. The peace of God, therefore, is the type and model of that peace which we must seek to establish among ourselves on earth.

Yet Jesus *is* our peace, not only as God, but also as the God-man, in virtue of that union (called hypostatic) effected in His person between His humanity and His divinity. Human nature—at best infinitely below the divine level, and in its fallen state shamefully stained and corrupted—is purified in Jesus and joined to the divine nature in a union so intimate and singular that there is simply no parallel to it in the whole universe. Therefore, just as it is true to say that Jesus is our "justification and sanctification and redemption" (7) precisely because of this union, so is it true to say, on the same account, that He is our peace, reconciling within His person our common humanity to God, sanctifying it by its union with the divine nature. Although this union as it is in Christ is unique, yet we

(6) Eph. 2, 14.
(7) I Cor. 1, 30.

are also in some manner to share it: as He, being divine, became a sharer in our humanity, so also we, through His humanity, are to become sharers in His divinity. In this marvelous way is peace re-established between God and fallen humanity. Elevated to the divine plane by grace, which is a participation in the divine life, men in this manner benefit by the peace won for them by Christ; participating in this peace, they are to reproduce within themselves, so far as this is possible, that union between humanity and divinity which finds its perfect realization in Christ; so that He is indeed our peace.

Finally, even in His humanity, Jesus *is* our peace: as Head of humanity He stands before God, not as a mere individual or the representative of a particular group, but in His essential humanity as Head of the whole race, the second Adam. Although He has a human nature, He has not an individual human personality. He gathers within Himself all the essential elements of human nature, but His personality is divine. How well, therefore, may He stand for all mankind! Through Him all are formed into one juridical society, united among themselves and represented before God as one body. Even to accept Jesus as their Head already brings men together in peace with one another.

The humanity of Jesus is also the means, or instrument, used by God to give peace to the world, just as it is the instrument of redemption. "For it has pleased God the Father . . . that through Him [Jesus] He should reconcile to Himself all things, whether on earth or in the heavens, *making peace through the blood of His cross.*" (8) The peace of Christ, like all the fruits of the redemption, was "bought at a great price." (9) This is why it is not to be obtained for society by such easy means as economic pacts, political alliances, or military victory. The order of means, once fixed by God, remains forever the same: in our day also, peace can be attained only through the humanity of Jesus and the blood of the cross. When men reject Jesus and refuse the burden of the cross, peace becomes for them an impossibility.

---

(8) Col. 1, 20.
(9) I Cor. 6, 20.

3. *In virtue of His office.* The office of Jesus is that of mediator between God and man, and His purpose is to establish and preserve peace between them. "For there is one God, and one mediator of God and men, the man Christ Jesus. . . ." (10) For this office He is peculiarly well fitted: being man, He can in truth be the representative of mankind at the divine court; being divine, His presence is acceptable to the Father. And so He works for us that we may have "peace with God." (11) Of course He "gave Himself a redemption *for all*," (12) and not for a few scattered individuals or any national or racial groups. In so doing, He intended to "break down the middle wall of partition" that had hitherto divided men and "reconcile both [that is, both Jews and Gentiles] to God in one body by the cross, killing the enmities in Himself." As a result of this, none will henceforth be "strangers and foreigners" but all will rather be "fellow citizens with the saints and the domestics of God." (13) Domestics of God, that is, of God's household, introduced and adopted into that wonderful harmony and peace that reigns in the Trinity! And this is for *all* —all peoples, all races, all classes, all nationalities. Such being God's design, men will henceforth fail to realize peace only through their own neglect or malice.

Accordingly, when as High Priest Jesus offers His eternal sacrifice, He does so in order to reconcile all men to the Father. This universality is so essentially characteristic of the priesthood of Jesus that He will not exercise it on our behalf unless we acknowledge the bond uniting us to one another. He will act for us only if we are together, gathered into the unity which He symbolizes and perfects: if we separate ourselves from our fellows, then His sacrifice is no longer ours, no longer for us. "If therefore thou offer thy gift at the altar, and there thou remember that thy brother hath anything against thee; leave there thy offering before the altar, and go first to be reconciled to thy brother, and then coming thou shalt offer

(10) I Tim. 2, 5.
(11) Rom. 5, 1.
(12) I Tim. 2, 6.
(13) Eph. 2, 14-19.

thy gift." (14) The reason for this? "Every one who hates his brother is a murderer, and you know that no murderer has eternal life abiding in him." (15) Before the law and the love of Christ all divisions among men must give way. All are one, united by love: "There is neither Jew nor Greek: there is neither bond nor free: there is neither male nor female. For you are all one in Christ Jesus." (16)

If the function of the priest is to sacrifice, the purpose of sacrifice itself is ultimately peace and love, the double peace between man and God and among men. So Christ expressed the matter in His final priestly prayer: "And not for them only [i.e., the Apostles] do I pray, but for them also who through their word shall believe in me: That they all may be one, as Thou, Father, in me, and I in Thee; that they all may be one in us. . . ." (17)

4. *Christ is our peace, finally, because of His example.* He did not speak of peace only when He entered the world and again when He left it. During His stay on earth He was also preoccupied with it; above all others, He was Himself a man of peace and walked the way of peace. He spent three years preaching the Gospel which Isaias and St. Paul called "the Gospel of Peace"; and the other thirty years of His life were spent in preparation for this great work. To John the Baptist, anxious to know whether He was in truth the Messias, Jesus gave as criterion of His divine mission the fact that "the poor have the Gospel preached to them." (18) It is indeed a pledge of the divine: "How beautiful are the feet of those who preach the Gospel of Peace; of those who bring glad tidings of good things." (19) How apt, too, is this Scriptural description of the message of Jesus! "And coming He *preached peace* to you that were afar off, and peace to them that were nigh. For by Him we have access both in one spirit to the Father." (20)

---

(14) St. Matt. 5, 23.
(15) I St. John 3, 15.
(16) Gal. 3, 28.
(17) St. John 17, 20-21.
(18) St. Matt. 11, 5.
(19) Rom. 10, 15.
(20) Eph. 2, 17-18.

Moreover He instructed His apostles to preach the same Gospel; and these, the Scriptures assure us, when Jesus had gone, went about "preaching peace by Christ Jesus." (21) The Master's directions in this matter had been explicit: "And when you come into the house salute it, saying: Peace be to this house. And if that house be worthy, your peace shall come upon it; but if it be not worthy, your peace shall return to you." (22)

The special and peculiar gift of Jesus Christ to men is peace: "Peace I leave with you, my peace I give unto you." (23) In the end, as has been observed, peacemaking wins for us adoption as children of God, according to the promise of the Beatitude, because it perfects our resemblance to the supreme Peacemaker, who was also the only-begotten Son of God. If we were to take the high vocation of Christian in all seriousness, as it certainly should be taken, the world would soon be full of peacemakers; and of peace.

5. This doctrine, before it is really accepted, must not only be admired for its great beauty, but must also be accepted in its practical implications. And practically, it requires that all peace efforts be made *with* and *in* and *through* Christ Jesus: *"Through Him and with Him and in Him, is to Thee, God the Father Almighty, in the unity of the Holy Spirit, all honor and glory."* (24) How this is to be done has been explained at length throughout these chapters and also in *Weapons of the Spirit.* At this point it is sufficient to recapitulate and summarize.

There are two aspects to the peace effort, one negative, the other positive. The negative task is the removal of obstacles to peace; the positive task is the actual creation of peace. Both are to be accomplished by specifically Christian means.

On the negative side, since the cause of war is spiritual—forgetfulness of God and the idolatry of creatures—the true remedy obviously is, not war, but the elimination of that cause, which can be accomplished only by a purely spiritual effort.

(21) Acts 10, 36.
(22) St. Matt. 10, 12-13.
(23) St. John 14, 27.
(24) From the Canon of the Mass.

Moreover, because this analysis of causes is certain, being given in the first place by divine revelation and repeated in our day and for our circumstances by the Vicar of Christ on earth, it is possible with great confidence, and indeed with certainty, to apply the proper spiritual remedies without need of having recourse to what are at best the crude and barbarous means of armed might, however justified (at the ethical level) such action might be. When war can be admitted as just, even ethically, only when it is *a last resort,* there is no reason why, with the deeper knowledge of causes and the more powerful means given to us by divine revelation, there should be resort to arms at all.

Catholics who, without hoping for too much from war, nevertheless concede to it a certain power to stop the spread of evil, must admit, in accordance with the traditional Scholastic doctrine, which has already been explained, that a just war cannot *directly* create peace or do any more than remove obstacles that stand in its way. (24a) And once we stand on the superior vantage point provided by revelation, from which the true causes of war are clearly revealed, it is impossible to escape the further conviction that the real, although unseen, obstacles to peace are best removed by spiritual means, while the shock of arms is powerless to touch them at all—much less able to eradicate them, which, however, is necessary if there is ever to be true and lasting peace.

On the positive side, peace itself, being a fruit of the spirit, can be introduced into the world only by cultivating the supernatural life and the essential virtue of charity. Thus from whichever side we view the matter—from the negative side which exposes the roots of conflict, or from the positive, which shows the way to true peace—it is clear and certain that war is not necessary, that it cannot reach the evil which it pretends

---

(24a) That is, *theoretically* war can do this. Here again, however, there is a great difference between theory and practice. Instead of removing injustice, war in reality consolidates and extends injustice, for it leads to settlements based on force rather than on justice, and dictated by greed, fear, hatred, revenge. The Treaty of Versailles is a classic example of this. Events indicate that World War II is moving towards the same kind of settlement.

to overcome, and that men can, therefore, perform their duties to their country more perfectly and more effectively by undertaking lives of holiness than by bearing arms.

In this way must we then set out to restore and re-establish *all things in Christ.* (25) According to Pope Pius XII (*Summi Pontificatus*), secularism—the divorce of human life and society from the influence of Christ—is one of the chief evils of our day. The decisions of States are based on self-interest, nationalistic ambition, expedience, power politics, and the immoral law of retaliation. The teachings of the Gospel, if they are noticed at all, are regarded as the expressions of a pretty sentiment having little relation to the realities of political life; nowhere are they the determining principles of action. A true Christian is shocked at this; he suffers inwardly, he weeps, he prays. Meanwhile, shall he acquiesce in the godless system? Shall he go along with its demands, hoping in the end to influence it for the good?

Shall he join the number of those who, sincerely regretting the fact that Christ is so universally ignored, nevertheless feel that since the world is not Christian, it would be unreasonable and inopportune to demand a settlement of world problems on evangelic principles? Shall he, with them, lay aside the Gospel for the time being and seek a solution on the basis of natural law, which should be acceptable to all men of reason, and not merely to Christians? No; the hopes of these men are doomed to end in nothing. *God has made the humanity of Christ the instrument through which all spiritual effects are to be accomplished. God owes it to the Humanity of His Son to make all efforts fail that are not centered in Him.* (26)

Further, not only will means that are not *in Christ Jesus* always prove ineffective from the practical point of view, but it must be added that we have not a right to use them either. If the world is not Christian, so much the worse for the world. It has not the right to ignore Christ; nor have Christians the right to pardon or acquiesce in its denial. And if, nevertheless,

(25) Eph. 1, 10.
(26) This principle is given by Dom Chautard, *The Soul of the Apostolate,* Part I, No. 2. (Gethsemane, Ky., The Trappist Press, 1941.)

the world persists in its course, then the Christian certainly has the right [and also, if he truly loves, an urgent need—*the charity of Christ constraineth us* (27)] to refuse to participate in any system that is not based on the true *Cornerstone* (28) or to engage in any efforts, however necessary they may be esteemed by others, that are not conducted *in Christ Jesus.* His participation in a godless world's affairs will be only such as is necessary to turn it to God.

---

(27) Col. 1, 16.
(28) Eph. 2, 20; II Cor. 5, 14.

XII

THE IMMACULATE QUEEN OF PEACE

I. Why Mary Is Truly Queen of Peace

The most imperious desire of the human heart, the philosophers say, is the desire for happiness; and yet "the man on the street," a distinguished observer has remarked, reveals in his countenance that he lives "a life of quiet desperation." Why this contradiction between fact and aspiration? Is there nothing in reality to correspond with the desire for happiness? If the longing for happiness is universal, so also the world offers its attractive fruits in abundance, and at no great cost, nor are they far to seek. "The world seems made for the enjoyment of just such a being as man, and man is put into it. He has the *capacity* of enjoyment, and the world supplies the *means*. How natural this, what a simple as well as pleasant philosophy. . . ." (1) The problem of happiness seems, at least on the surface, and to most men, to offer no special difficulty; and how few there are who do not grasp at this easy but disappointing solution!

That is exactly the trouble: this solution is too easy, too superficial. Thoughtful men quickly reject it—even thoughtless men come at the end to experience its folly. It leads to emptiness, disillusionment, bitterness, despair. The fruit that the world offers, fair to behold, is disappointing to the taste: always it is insipid, often it is bitter, sometimes it is deadly. "The world is sweet to the lips, but bitter to the taste. It pleases at first, but not at last. It looks gay on the outside, but evil and misery lie concealed within. When a man has passed a certain number of years in it, he cries out with the Preacher, 'Vanity of vanities, all is vanity'." (2)

These last words, spoken by a very saintly Christian, are

(1) Newman, Parochial and Plain Sermons, Vol. VII, Sermon VI.
(2) Newman, *ibid.*

likely to be regarded by the worldly-minded as "a gloomy view of things." Worldlings, however bitter their experience, will not accept such a judgment; and their protest is once and for all fixed in the words which a modern pagan poet put in the dying lips of an ancient pagan emperor: "Thou hast conquered, O pale Galilean, and the world has grown gray with thy breath." Yet the point of these words, aside from the blasphemy, is that even the pagan acknowledges the victory of Christ—a victory which is not only that of a divine person over mere man, but also of the eternal Truth over an inadequate and deceitful philosophy. It is Christ's doctrine that the pagan hates, His doctrine of the Cross, which cuts right across the pleasure philosophy. "If any man would be my disciple, let him deny himself and take up his cross daily and follow me." (3) To a man whose deepest aspirations are satisfied by food or the dainties of the flesh, or who seeks to satisfy them so, the person and teaching of Jesus cannot be other than offensive. Still, the pagan must concede the victory to Christianity. He is forced to admit, in spite of himself, that his pleasant philosophy of living does not work in the end and cannot be finally acceptable to the human heart. All his songs are filled with the sadness of this admission:

> "At a touch sweet Pleasure melteth,
> Like to bubbles when rain pelteth;
>
> ....
>
> O sweet Fancy! let her loose;
> Summer's joys are spoilt by use,
> And the enjoying of the Spring
> Fades as does its blossoming:
> Autumn's red-lipped fruitage too,
> Blushing through the mist and dew,
> Cloys with tasting...
>
> ....
>
> O sweet Fancy! let her loose;
> Everything is spoilt by use..."

(3) St. Luke 9, 23.

The popularity of taverns, and the prevalence of alcoholism, to say nothing of the other excesses of the flesh, are unmistakable evidence that, while sensualists are all forced to recognize with Keats the inadequacy of earthly joys, they are nevertheless not satisfied with his solution, which is to "let the fancy loose" and enjoy the refined and fragile pleasures of imagination. Most men want more substantial comfort.

Yet even those who are more spiritually minded suffer a similar disappointment. With a more elevated view of life, knowing that true happiness is a thing of the spirit and does not consist in mere sensual delight, they are nevertheless frequently embittered by the human disappointments which they experience. Their days are filled with trials and afflictions. Providence treats them no better than sinners; indeed, if the Scriptures are to be believed, they are treated worse than sinners: "whom the Lord loveth, He chastiseth." (4) The carnal mind could not of course be expected to understand that true happiness is given, not to those that laugh, but to those that mourn. The sad and strange thing is that even Christians do not understand it. If they reject the view that happiness is in sensual pleasure, they are human enough to believe, like the pagan philosophers, that a certain amount of this world's goods is necessary for happiness; and they suffer from the afflictions that deprive them of these goods or embitter the possession of them. They need a stronger spirit of faith and abandonment to the decrees of Providence in their behalf before they will learn *by experience,* and not merely from a book, that blessedness is indeed for the meek and for those that mourn.

If we go from the average imperfect Christian to the saints we will scarcely find their experience more encouraging to the human spirit. Their lives without exception illustrate the truth of that strange saying that the Lord chastises whom He loves. Afflicted by life-long and painful maladies, they suffer also persecutions, calumnies, misunderstandings, contradictions of all kinds. Their work is constantly harried by those who should be the first to support it; they are the most fiercely op-

(4) Heb. 12, 6.

posed by those whom they seek to benefit. In addition to this, they go through dark interior trials, dryness, desolation, terrifying temptations. These last trials, the most painful of all, the ordinary man knows nothing about except by report; but these reports, when read, although not even then fully understood, are likely to leave one in a state of mind similar to that experienced in reading horror stories at dead of night, alone.

The drift of these remarks and their connection with the Queen of Peace will be apparent after we have formulated the truth and principle that is revealed in them. It is this: man cannot in this world achieve happiness on the sense level because he is higher than a sensual being; and he cannot possess spiritual and supernatural happiness except he undergo a preliminary purification that is most painful for the natural man. *As he is*—with his fallen nature, poisoned by the threefold concupiscence—*he is not fit for happiness.* Similarly he is not fit for those things that go with happiness; he is not fit for joy, true joy of spirit, which is a gift of the Spirit; *he is not fit, as he is, to receive peace,* which is also a gift of the Spirit. This is why men, despite the intensity of their desire for happiness, rarely achieve it. It is why, despite their longing for peace, they do not obtain it. They try to get these goods without the trouble and pain of purification. They forget that true happiness is spiritual and supernatural; or, if they remember this, then they forget that they must be purified to receive it.

Here also is the reason why faithful Christians needs must suffer more than sinners, why the saints suffer most of all. Suffering and painful trial, besides being used by God as a punishment for the wicked, is used also as a purification of the good. St. Peter compares the just man to gold and silver, which are purified by fire. (5) Suffering—bodily or mental, natural or supernatural—is the fire by which Providence purges those who have not yet reached perfection and prepares them to become fellow-citizens of the saints.

God regards all merely natural and sensual attachments to the creatures of the world as impurities, and He removes these

(5) I St. Peter 1, 6-7.

from the soul in two ways, by demanding mortification and by inflicting trials. Suffering is nothing else than the privation of some good thing to which we are attached in a manner that is too human and selfish; as when a man is separated from the money he loves by some business failure. Suffering differs from mortification only in this, that in the latter we deprive ourselves of earthly pleasures, whereas in the former it is God Himself, by His providential control of all the events in the world, who takes them from us. In either case the purpose is the same: to empty the heart of carnal affections and prepare it for the love of God. Because God requires our total and exclusive love, He regards jealously all affections that we direct to creatures apart from Him and He seeks to break them off one at a time by the afflictions He sends us. To love God wholly we must be purified of a merely natural love for creatures; and once to love God so is to hold all creatures in contept. "Was she so very beautiful?" Bernadette was asked after the Blessed Virgin had appeared to her at Lourdes. "So beautiful," was the reply, "that when one has once seen her, one cannot love anything else on earth." Bernadette came to detachment and contempt of worldly goods through the apparition granted in her youth. All of us, like Bernadette, must first learn the nothingness of the world and then, by painful experience, submit to being detached from all its goods.

From these facts two important conclusions are to be drawn. First of all, peace cannot be realized unless men undergo a profound purification. As sanctification is necessary, so also is purification; indeed the latter is but the under side, the shadowed side, of the former, and men can advance in holiness only in so far as they are purified of the dross of earthly affections by voluntary renunciation and willing submission to the trials arranged by a loving Providence. Doomed in advance are all those philosophies and systems which seek peace, or in any other way attempt to provide for human happiness, without taking into account this need for purification and man's incapacity for happiness *as he now is.* For sensual happiness is not real—at least it is not substantial or lasting; it is a thing of the surface. If opponents of the Church deride the Christians' other-worldliness (would that more of them were in truth other-worldly!) they themselves, with all the technical achievements of the modern world at their disposal, have not been able to bring to men even material happiness. In fact, precisely through these means, they have multiplied misery. Thus it is that men cannot enjoy for long even the false, sensual peace that comes of possessing earthly goods; they are so greedy that they destroy one another in grabbing for these goods. As for true peace, being a by-product of the love of God, it can be possessed only by the clean of heart. It is to be understood why atheists do not act on this truth; they do not know it. What is to be lamented is that Catholics forget it and in planning for peace draw up programs, adopt resolutions, publish recommendations, and form organizations as though the Doctrine of the Fall of Man had been deleted from the Catechism.

The second corollary to be drawn from these facts is that true devotion to Our Lady, the most pure Virgin, *Virgo purissima,* is an integral and necessary part of the Christian peace effort. Let it be noted that Our Lady's importance here, as in the plan of salvation generally, is doctrinal and not sentimental. Being part of the *order of means* fixed eternally by Almighty God to obtain *all* graces and spiritual benefits, her assistance is surely necessary to obtain the peace of God. It behooves us, therefore, to understand the doctrinal foundations for the position given her in the Providential plan. To call her Queen of Peace is not just to add to a picturesque but empty enumeration of meaningless titles. Each title of Our Lady describes one of the many matchless prerogatives that have been conferred upon her. To call her Queen of Peace is to designate a prerogative, a dignity, a power, conferred on her by God Himself. This title directs our attention to the fact that only through her will the world be filled with peacemakers, will we ourselves become true and effective peacemakers, will her Son's kingdom of peace be established on this earth. A queen is one who rules. If Mary is Queen of Peace, she rules over peace; its treasury is in her hands. To seek entrance into the kingdom of peace is to enter her domain; to work for the coming of the kingdom of peace is to place one's self under her authority.

Blessed Grignon de Montfort (6), quoting St. Augustine, shows why Mary has a principal part in spreading the Gospel of peace. "The world was unworthy to receive the Son of God immediately from the Father's hands. He has given Him to Mary in order that the world might receive Him through her."

Here, in one of the marvelous intuitions of the saints, you have the reason why Mary is *needed* in the divine economy; the reason, also, why she is needed to obtain peace. Because of our impurity, the result of the Fall, we could not have peace, which is a gift of the Spirit. More than that, because of our impurity, we could not have Jesus Himself except through her. She alone, immaculately conceived and remaining sinless throughout her life, can be the means of bringing Him into the world. She alone, therefore, can be the means of transmitting to the world the peace which is His gift.

Since Mary was to come into such close contact with divinity, she needed to be the wholly pure. Since He who was holiness itself was to come among us, only one without blemish could bring Him into a world that is so filled with sin. With Him, as He comes, Jesus brings all that men desire—joy, wisdom, happiness, peace. For these things the world reaches out eagerly. Alas, it cannot take them. They are spiritual, while the world is deeply infected with sin: are pearls to be given to swine? Despite our longings it would appear that our sinfulness will cheat us of ever realizing our deepest and best aspirations. But lo, she comes—our Mother as well as His; having no spot or impurity, she takes without impropriety, without presumption, what we dare not, cannot, touch. As a mother puts aside family heirlooms to save them for her children, so does Mary receive our inheritance into her custody, keeping for us the gifts that Jesus brings. See, she holds the Prince of Peace. She holds also, in custody, His gift of peace. What He brings we may receive through her.

---

(6) *True Devotion to the Blessed Virgin Mary.* (Bay Shore, N. Y.; The Montfort Fathers.)

But when? Is she alone to possess it? Are we not to share it at all? Is our impurity, our imperfection, to stand forever between us and "the most beautiful of all gifts"?

No. Besides keeping this gift for us, Mary also shows us how to obtain it. She holds it for us until we are prepared to receive it, helping us at the same time to get prepared. As the mother, having saved the ancient and precious heirlooms, gives them over to her children when these are grown up and able to appreciate their value, so Mary will give us the spiritual goods destined for us by our Father in heaven when we have ceased from our carnal ways and become spiritual-minded. Moreover, her character, her life, her dispositions, are the lesson to us of what we must become if we wish to approach the God-man and stretch forth our hands to receive His gifts. It is by reproducing within ourselves, so far as this can be done, the interior life of Mary, which brought God to her, that we can have Him also come to us. By sharing in her dispositions we will attract the Spirit of Jesus to our souls as she did to hers, winning God himself as her Spouse. We must learn her secret if we would share her grace. Otherwise . . . "one of the great reasons why the Holy Ghost does not now do startling wonders in our souls is because He does not find there a sufficiently great union with His faithful and inseparable spouse." (7)

If Peace is one of the twelve fruits of the Holy Spirit, here is the way that He can be induced to come among us and bestow His gift. "When the Holy Ghost, her Spouse, has found Mary in a soul, He flies there, He enters there in His fullness; He communicates Himself to that soul abundantly, and to the full extent to which she makes room for her Spouse." (8)

By Mary, therefore, and through Mary, can men overcome the heavy handicap that hinders them in their work for individual and social happiness. If they are now, as they are, not fit to possess happiness and peace, they need not despair. They can become fit. Our Lady will show them how it is to be done, how they may set about purifying and preparing their souls.

(7) *Ibid.*
(8) *Ibid.*

This is the great and arduous preliminary task that must be done before the world can receive peace, the "pearl of great price." Here also is the manner in which it is to be accomplished.

Yet if Mary were only an example, a model to us, we might well despair. The privilege of her Immaculate Conception places her so far beyond us, that of ourselves we could not think of imitating her virtue. But because Mary is our mother, she not only tells us what we must do, but helps us to do it, supporting every step. Her Immaculate Conception, high as it was, was the result of divine grace; as our mother, she will see that we in turn obtain the grace needed to become her pure children.

"It is with her, in her, and of her, that He [the Holy Spirit] has produced His masterpiece, which is a God made man." But this does not end the work of the Divine Artist. If Christians are to be like Christ, conformed to Christ, other Christs, this also is the work of the Holy Spirit and He accomplishes it, as He forms the God-man, through Mary; it is through Mary that He "goes on producing [Jesus] in the persons of His members daily to the end of the world. The predestinate are the members of that adorable Head. This is the reason why He, the Holy Ghost, the more He finds Mary, His dear and inseparable spouse, in any soul, becomes the more active and mighty in producing Jesus Christ in that soul, and that soul in Jesus Christ." (9)

Men can realize the high ideals of the Sermon on the Mount, they can walk according to the pattern of life set down there by Jesus, only if they are other Christs. What is required is no mere human righteousness or respectability, it is divine holiness; we are to become perfect as our heavenly Father is perfect. To achieve such comduct, Christ must act in us and through us. It must be, with us, as it was with St. Paul, that *we no longer live but Christ lives in us.* Then will we also be able to say, with the same saint, that we can do all things through Him who strengthens us. Jesus in us will make us

(9) *Ibid.*

poor in spirit, meek, loving towards our enemies, ready to turn the other cheek, rejoicing in tribulation. Jesus living in us will also make us peacemakers.

In this way can we have a Christian society, for in this way will we have true Christians. Only in this way, let us add: only if Jesus lives in us will we be able to rebuild the world on the plan set forth in the Sermon on the Mount. Only then will we realize that dream of Pope Pius XI, "the Peace of Christ in the reign of Christ."

And it is through Mary that all this is to be done, for it is through Mary that the Holy Spirit—and only He can do it—will reproduce Jesus in our souls. More appropriately than St. Paul she can cry out, "My little children, I am in labor again until Christ be formed in you." As Christ, the Supreme Peacemaker, reconciling earth to heaven and all men to one another, came to us through her, so likewise it is through her that the Holy Spirit will form all the members of His body into peacemakers. In bringing Jesus to birth in us, she also enables us to attain to that climactic achievement of the beatitudes, peacemaking, which making us children of God, thereby unites us in true brotherhood to Him who, while the only-begotten Son of God, was also the "first-born of many brethren." (10)

2. The Meaning of the Immaculate Heart

What is required, in particular, is devotion to Mary's purity, to her Immaculate Heart. The purity of Our Lady gives her special prerogatives in regard to peace. For this reason Pope Pius XII, in his great desire for peace, consecrated, during World War II, the whole world to the Immaculate Heart of Mary. Let us take time to inquire the reason for this; so that we may know the meaning of Mary's purity and realize what devotion to her Immaculate Heart demands of us.

Purity is frequently spoken of as though it were the same as chastity. Yet it is not so: the virtue of purity is higher and holier even than chastity. Accordingly, it is not just the avoid-

(10) Rom. 8, 29.

ance of sexual sin; it is not only the guarding of bodily integrity; it is not merely the renunciation of all sexual love, including that which is legitimate and sanctioned by holy wedlock. To chastity, rather, belongs the regulation of sex, whether in the married or the unmarried. Hence chastity is "a virtue whose positive quality is created by the avoidance of something negative. In man, chastity, as we can easily understand, is at once a presupposition and a result of purity, but it covers a far more restricted ground. It is concerned exclusively with sex, and consists *solely* in a right attitude towards sex, whereas purity consists in a more general response to value. The symbol of the latter is not the protective girdle or the fortress which secludes and guards, but unsullied whiteness, the lily, unclouded light." (11)

Although of course purity does, in the first place, "imply and demand a particular attitude towards sex," nevertheless, unlike chastity, it does not consist "primarily and necessarily in an attitude towards sex, but *primarily in an abiding in God's presence and a surrender to the glory of His countenance.*" (12)

There you have it: purity is a *complete* stainlessness which at once enables its possessors to approach the All-Holy God and is the result of His presence. It does not free the soul from the corruption of sexual concupiscence only, but also from all the manifold forms of concupiscence and sensuality. It is the preservation, not only of the flesh from carnal sin, but of the heart's affections, intact, for God alone; it is a refusal to surrender one's love, *in however small a measure,* to any creature apart from God. It is, therefore, the "reflected splendor of God's light shining in the soul." (13) The countenance of the pure is a mirror in which the presence of God is reflected. You may see this in the face of a saint, for example, St. Teresa of Lisieux, and even in the face of a child, who, as Newman says, "has this one great gift, *that he seems to have lately come from God's presence,* and not to understand the language of this

(11) *In Defense of Purity,* by Dietrich von Hildebrand, p. 69. (New York: Sheed & Ward, 1935).
(12) *Ibid.,* p. 70. Italics ours.
(13) *Ibid.,* p. 79.

visible scene, or how it is a temptation, how it is a veil interposing itself between the soul and God." (14)

Mary's purity, therefore, as distinct from her perfect chastity, was a complete surrender of her heart to God, a freedom from the slightest imperfection that would come of loving creatures sensually or for their own sakes. Her heart is pure because it is holy; it is holy because it is free from every desire except the desire for God. Her love for Joseph, sincere and great, the model of pure love for all Christian spouses, was centered in God and motivated entirely by love for Him; hence, it subtracted nothing from her love for God, but rather added to this, being the occasion for her daily meriting new growths in divine love. Our Lady "well knew that God does not accept a divided heart, but wills that, as He has commanded, it should be consecrated to His love without the least reserve: Thou shalt love the Lord thy God with thy whole heart. Hence from the first moment of her life she began to love God with all her strength, and gave herself entirely to Him. . . ." (15)

Mary's spirit was that of the dove. "At the time of the Deluge a raven sent out of the ark by Noah remained to feed on dead bodies; but the dove, without resting her foot, quickly 'returned to him in the ark.' Many who are sent by God into this world unfortunately remain to feed on earthly goods. It was not thus that Mary, our heavenly dove, acted; she knew full well that God should be our only hope, our only love; she knew that the world is full of dangers, and that he who leaves it soonest is freest from its snares." (16)

Because the only love that Mary knew was for her God, her heart was immaculate. And it is easily to be seen, from what has been said in earlier chapters, why this purity fits her to be Queen of Peace. Her heart, filled only with supernatural love, cannot but abound in peace, which is the effect and fruit of that love. The fullness of her love, commensurate with the fullness of her grace, gives her also the fullness of peace. And,

---

(14) Cardinal Newman, *Parochial and Plain Sermons*, Vol. II, p. 65.
(15) St. Alphonsus de Liguori, *The Glories of Mary*, p. 342. (Brooklyn, N. Y.: The Redemptorist Fathers, 1931.)
(16) *Ibid.*, p. 341.

as she dispenses all the divine favors, so she possesses peace, not only for herself, but also to distribute to her children on earth.

Yet to receive peace from Mary commits us to striving for the purity of Mary. She shows us what must happen to our hearts, how they must be emptied and cleansed and scoured, if they are to become receptacles of peace. You see then what is necessary if we are to practice true devotion to the Immaculate Heart of Mary! It is rather more than burning votive candles in front of a shrine with that name, while we live as we please, according to our caprice and sensual desires! Indeed, true devotion cannot exist in men whose hearts are filled with earthly desires and affections; or if it is attempted, it will be only a worthless externalism, a pretense, hypocrisy. This is why Mary, although Queen of Peace, is unable, in spite of all our prayers to her, to give us peace: not because she is powerless, but because our hearts are so filled with vain and perhaps sinful affections that we are unable to receive that peace which is distilled from divine love. "When my Immaculate Heart triumphs," said Our Lady to the children at Fatima, "the world will have peace."

3. The Three Messages of Mary

With the foregoing truths in mind, it can scarcely seem surprising that Our Lady was the one chosen by God to bear a special message of peace to the modern world. Three times, in fact, in miraculous apparitions that have been authenticated by the most exacting tribunals, Our Lady has appeared with a divine message for our unhappy world. Each time she has spoken to us through innocent and ingenuous children, just as she herself had formerly been chosen by God to bring His Son into the world because of her innocence.

The first apparition was in 1846 and took place in France on the mountain of La Salette. Our Lady appeared to two cowherds, a boy and a girl, while they were watching their herds in the fields. She was weeping. In what Leon Bloy has called "the most redoubtable canticle that mankind has heard since the Magnificat," (17) she deplored the sins of her people and spoke of the difficulty she was having in restraining the hand of her Son. There was reference to local blasphemies and irreligion, together with prophecies as to the punishment that would follow upon them. But there was also, as in Christ's prophecies in the Scripture, a larger reference to the affairs of the whole world. Our Lady was weeping over the sins of all her people, and predicting the dread punishments that would come if there were not a change in their way of life. The children therefore were commissioned by her to "make this to be known to all my people."

To each of the children the Lady communicated a secret. In accordance with her instructions, these were never revealed to anyone except to Pope Pius IX, at his command. It is not known exactly what they are, but it is thought, from external indications, that they refer to coming world events and impending punishments. "From bits of information that have fallen, as well as from observations made on the general conduct of the children with reference to their secrets, it is generally at this day understood that . . . Maximin's secret announces mercy and the rehabilitation of things, whilst Melanie's announces great chastisements. . . ." (18)

Pope Pius IX, after reading the secrets, said, "These are scourges with which France is threatened, but she is not alone culpable. Germany, Italy, all Europe is culpable and merits chastisement. . . ." (19) When the Pope was asked later to reveal these secrets, he replied, "You wish to know the secrets of La Salette? Well, here are the secrets of La Salette: Unless you do penance, you shall all perish."

This summary by the Pope can be taken as final and authoritative and, quite apart from the secrets, it epitomizes the whole message of Our Lady to the children. This was God's first solemn warning to the modern world—a world which, wholly

---

(17) Leon Bloy, speaking through Marchenoir, in "*The Woman Who Was Poor*" (New York: Sheed & Ward.)

(18) *The Holy Mountain of La Salette*, by the Most Rev. Wm. Ullathorne, p. 99. (Altamont, N. Y.: La Salette Press.)

(19) *Ibid.*, p. 100.

irreligious and confident of itself, was moving rapidly to its own destruction. It was the great nineteenth century, the age of scientific discovery and material prosperity, at this time nearing the peak of its achievement. It was nearing also the climax of its neglect of God; and in those days, when men were so lost in admiration of their own works and were talking wildly of the universal peace and prosperity that they would achieve by means of "science" without God and in contempt of Him—in those days it could be clearly seen *only in heaven* that the nineteenth century plans for a materialistic paradise on earth were not, as claimed, a solid promise of science, but a fantastic and blasphemous dream that was soon to bring men to a condition of misery and suffering hitherto unknown. At La Salette came God's warning. "I can assure you that that spot is especially frequented by the Thunders of the Apocalypse, and that there is no other spot on earth where those can go who are interested in the final culmination of the Redemption. At La Salette and nowhere else can you be fortified if you are aware that *all things are not fulfilled* and that the High Mass of the Comforter has not yet begun. . . ." (20)

The second apparition came in 1858, to Bernadette, a child of Lourdes. To her also Our Lady appeared, altogether eighteen times, speaking to her and reciting the Rosary with her. Although Bernadette was made marvelously happy by the vision, she was also often saddened by the messages confided to her care. At the eighth apparition, for example, "the ever-growing crowd noted again the radiant smile which denoted the advent of the Lady, and the waves of sadness which from time to time broke upon the tranquillity of their communion. This time, perhaps, the note of sadness prevailed. Her arms fell listless to her sides, and tears streamed down her cheeks. She crept on her knees up the slope, kissing the ground in abject humility as she went, and prostrated herself finally below the eglantine. She looked up and listened, and then, turning with a sigh towards the crowd, murmured in a voice which but few could hear: "Penance! Penance! Penance!" (21)

(20) Leon Bloy, *op. cit.*, p. 88.
(21) *St. Bernadette*, L. L. McReavy, pp. 57-58. (St. Louis: Herder.)

Penance! Penance! Penance! Here is the second warning, an echo of the cry from La Salette, another motherly appeal to save her children. The significance of these words from the grotto of Lourdes—words which best summarize the message of Lourdes—is seen more clearly from an incident that occurred during one of the earlier apparitions. Bernadette "spoke also of a strange incident which had occurred during the vision. While she was at prayer, she said, a hubbub of sinister voices, rising apparently from the bowels of the earth, had broken out over the waters of the Gave, challenging, crossing, and clashing with each other, like the uproar of a brawling mob. One of these voices, towering above the rest, had cried in jarring, angry tones: 'Flee! Flee to safety!' At this cry, uttered in the tone of a menace, the Lady had raised her head and looked towards the river with a frown. It was but a simple movement, but it had sufficed to drive terror into the voices, and scatter them in every direction." (22)

In this way did the diabolic voices protest against the appearance of Our Lady, seeking to remove Bernadette (and the world!) from her influence. This was the Lady who, according to prophecy, was to crush the head of the serpent: at her mere frown the devil was forced to retreat.

Those diabolical voices are still heard all over the world. They are easily recognizable because they are so harsh, jangling, terrifying. They incite the greed which so disturbs and tortures our age; they create dissensions, so well known to us, over material goods; they originate and cry abroad slogans of hatred and revenge and war. They have caused once Christian nations to turn their backs on God and revert to the grossest materialism. They speak and spread the maxims of the *black paganism* condemned by Pius XII and written, not only in the text-books of Nazism and Fascism, but also, as the Pontiff said, in the worldliness of newspapers, magazines, radios, moving pictures, in the immodesty of styles, in the modern cult of the nude, the love of sensuality and impurity, the complete abandonment of men today to worldly pursuits and vanities. Our

(22) *Ibid.*, p. 44.

struggle is indeed not against "flesh and blood, but against the principalities and powers, against the world-rulers of this darkness, against the spiritual forces of wickedness on high." (23) It is these *world-rulers of darkness,* the very devils themselves, who have deluded men into taking up the search for material goods, have thereby set them at one another's throats, and have so successfully realized in our day, by means of global war, the dark ambition of spreading everywhere their dread kingdom of hatred, revenge, and evil. As with Bernadette, their voices warn us to flee from the Immaculate Conception and her influence.

If only men would obey that appeal for penance, as promptly and as literally as Bernadette! Then might we also induce this powerful Lady to frown in our behalf and disperse the furious rabble that goes about the world seeking whom it may devour.

The latest apparition was that of Fatima in Portugal. It happened in 1917 during World War I, and Our Lady's message was this time directly concerned with war and peace. Again she appeared to children, this time to three little shepherds, two girls and a boy, while they were tending their sheep. She urged upon them mortification, sacrifice, and particularly the proper recitation of the Rosary. This was to be done for the ending of the war, *"since she alone could bring it about."* (24)

During the third apparition (there were six altogether), Our Lady said, "I am the Lady of the Rosary and I have come to warn the faithful to amend their lives and ask pardon for their sins." (25) She also said that if people but amended their lives, the war would soon end. And she added that if this warning should not be heeded, another and a more terrible war would break out during the next Pontificate.

The great lessons that Mary taught at Fatima were the need of pardon for sins, the need of mortification and sacrifice, of conversion of heart and amendment of life. From this peace

---

(23) Eph. 6, 12.
(24) *Our Lady of Fatima,* by Msgr. Finbar Ryan, O.P., p. 57. (Westminster, Md.: The Newman Bookshop, 1944.)
(25) *Ibid.,* p. 73.

would result. The Rosary, recited daily, was the means insisted upon for obtaining all these spiritual goods.

The particular devotion which stems from Fatima is that to the Immaculate Heart of Mary. Lucia—the only one of the three children who heard Our Lady speak, and who is still living today in a convent in Portugal—said that they were told "to offer their prayers and sacrifices in reparation for sins committed against the Immaculate Heart of Mary." They were also given particular practices for this devotion. Less than thirty years afterwards, in the midst of World War II, Pope Pius XII, hearkening to the appeal of Our Lady of Fatima and remembering her promises of peace, consecrated the whole world to her Immaculate Heart.

Only, alas, how many refuse that consecration! How many by their manner of life make a mockery of it even while pronouncing its words! What is implied and demanded by this devotion has already been explained. If we meet these demands—on Our Lady's own words—the reward will be peace. But if we do not meet them? Then her answer is that of La Salette: "If my people will not submit, I shall be forced to let go the hand of my Son. It is so strong, so heavy, that I can no longer withhold it." Today we know by experience the weight of her Son's hand.

Prayer to the Queen of Peace

"Queen of the Most Holy Rosary, Refuge of the Human Race, Victress in all God's battles, we humbly prostrate ourselves before thy throne, confident that we shall receive mercy, grace and bountiful assistance and protection in the present calamity, not through our own inadequate merits, but solely through the great goodness of thy Maternal Heart. . . .

"May the sight of the widespread material and moral destruction, of the sorrows and anguish of countless fathers and mothers, husbands and wives, brothers and sisters, and innocent children, of the great number of lives cut off in the flower of youth, of the bodies mangled in horrible slaughter, and of the tortured and agonized souls in danger of being lost eternally, move thee to compassion!

"O Mother of Mercy, obtain peace for us from God, and above all procure for us those graces which prepare, establish and assure the peace!

"Queen of Peace, pray for us and give to the world now at war the peace for which all peoples are longing, peace in the truth, justice and charity of Christ. Give peace to the warring nations and to the souls of men, that in the tranquillity of order the Kingdom of God may prevail. . . ."

—*From Pope Pius XII's Act of Consecration of the Human Race to the Immaculate Heart of Mary. This consecration was made on November* 7, 1942, *the twenty-fifth anniversary of the apparitions at Fatima.*

PATRISTICS AND PEACE

An Appendix

The following extracts from the writings of the Fathers and Doctors of the Church were compiled for the Catholic Worker (June, 1943) by a member of the Catholic Pacifists Association of Canada.

FAITHFUL to merely human philosophy, the rationalist doctrine in Mein Kampf is that: "Pacifism is the deadliest sin, for Pacifism means the surrender of the Race in its fight for existence. The first duty of every country is, therefore, to nationalize the masses. . . . Without brute force it is impossible to ensure the survival of the Race." (Not the human race, of course.) "Hence the necessity for militarism." Faithful to this philosophy also is Fascism: "A doctrine which is founded upon this harmful postulate of peace is hostile to Fascism." (*Encyclopedia Italiana,* 1932.) Not so with Catholicism, however. This would be for Catholics a new kind of Conscientious Objection. Throughout the ages Evangelic Pacifism is not condemned as the deadliest sin, notwithstanding the fact that warfare is sometimes justified by ethics of strict justice and right which do not take into consideration the words of Christ: "Do not also the heathens this?" (St. Matt. 5:47, 6:32.)

Is Slaughter Innocent?

ST. ISIDORE PELUSIOT (d. 434): "Therefore I say that slaughter of enemies in wars may seem to be legitimate as much as you like, and monuments erected to the victorious, preaching their illustrious crimes; nevertheless, if the accurate and supreme understanding of the brotherhood among all men be had, this way indeed they will not seem to be so plainly innocent." (*Epist. CC, Ophelio Grammatico.*)

"A hard rumor has perturbed me, announcing certain things unhappy and to be detested. Some declare you to be so insane and affected by error of mind, that you would lead that young man . . . to arms and to that vile, despicable and outstanding school of death, the army. On account of which, if you have not already done so . . . desist from this preposterous counsel. Do not extinguish a lamp that struggles excellently to be lighted; but permit him who has use of reason to give assiduous work to studies. . . . As to that dignity, however (the army), or rather that dishonor and infamy, conciliate it with others, as free-booters, with whom common heartlessness and ingorance is connected." (*Epistolarum Lib. I,CCCXC—Quintiniano.*)

ST. CYRIL OF ALEXANDRIA (d. 430): "We are taught that we ought to be meek and pacific, and to take care by all means to go through life without fighting, 'For the servant of the Lord must not wrangle, but be mild towards all men,' as it is written (II Tim. 2: 24). . . . Indeed, by so thinking and doing, we shall gain the benefits which come from peace, and convert to benignity those who fought against us. 'For even the wild beasts shall be pacific with thee' (Job 5:23) . . . For peace is better than riches, and the possession of temporal goods is to be set aside for the sake of fraternal love." (*Glaphyrorum in Genesim, Lib. V. Cap. II*:2.)

ST. JOHN CHRYSOSTOM (d. 400): "That they may now understand that this is a new kind of warfare and not the usual custom of joining in battle, when He sent them with nothing He said: 'And so, marching on, show forth the meekness of lambs, although you are to go to wolves . . . for so will I best show my power, when the wolves are conquered by the lambs' . . . For certainly it is a greater work and much more marvelous to change the minds of opponents and to bring about a change of soul than to kill them. . . . We ought to be ashamed, therefore, who act far differently when as wolves we rush upon our adversaries. For as long as we are lambs we conquer; even when a thousand wolves stand about, we overcome and are victors. But if we act like wolves we are conquered, for then the aid of the Good Shepherd departs from us, for He does not foster wolves but sheep." (In Matt. Hom. 34, n.1:—Breviary, June 11th, Lesson IX.)

"There are three kinds of wars. There is the common war,

when soldiers are attacked by enemies; the second, when even in peace time we fight one another; the third, when each one wages war against himself. And this one is the gravest of all. Indeed, the war of the enemies cannot harm us much; what, indeed, I ask you, could they do? They strangle, they kill, but the soul they cannot harm. And neither will the second war be able to bring harm to us when we do not will it. For even if others should attack us with war, it is licit for us to remain in peace; indeed, hear the prophet saying: 'For that in which they should have loved me, they detracted me; but I prayed' (Ps. 108:4), again: 'With them that hated peace I was pacific' (Ps. 119:7), and again: 'When I was speaking to them they fought against me without cause' (Ps. 108:3)." *In Epist. Ia ad Timotheum, Homilia VII.*)

ST. MARTIN OF TOURS (397): "A soldier of Christ I am; to fight is not allowable for me."

Call Our Enemies Brothers

ST. GREGORY NAZIANZEN (d. 390): "This is the reward of sin to me. . . . Thence was avidity born; from avidity, cupidity; from cupidity, wars; from wars, moreover, taxations. . . . But we at least, let us not augment the penalty, since we are obnoxious to such punishment, nor let us fare harmfully with the others. From us, God demands mutual benignity towards one another, even if we receive that punishment from Him." (*Orat.* 19.)

"Let us venerate the mandate of the pacific; that is, peace, which, departing hence, He bequeathed to us as a legacy (St. John 14:27). Let us acknowledge but this one war, that which is committed with the adverse powers. As to those who have attacked us, let us call even them by the name of brothers. . . . Let us concede something somewhat small, that we might receive that which is greater, assuredly, concord. Let us suffer to be conquered, that we may conquer." (*Orat.* 22.)

ST. CYPRIAN (d. 304): "The earth is drenched with mutual bloodshed, and homicide which individuals commit is a crime; it is called virtue when it is waged publicly. It is not reason of innocence that acquires impunity for misdeeds, but enormity of crime." (*Epist. I ad Donat.*)

ORIGEN (d. 240): "Then Celsus exhorts us 'that we bring support to the king with all our powers, that we come into our share of his just labors, that we take up arms for him and, if he so require, that we militate under him, and that we conduct the army.' To these things it must be said that we give support to the king in due place, but godly support, as I should so say, shielded with the armor of God (Eph. 6:11); and this we do obeying this apostolic word: 'I urge, therefore, first of all, that supplications, prayers, intercessions and thanksgiving be made for all men, and for kings, and for all in high positions' (I Tim. 2:11); and inasmuch as one stands out the more in godliness, that much more does he give help to kings more powerfully; and he does more than the soldiers going out in battle array who kill enemy soldiers, as many of them as they are able. Furthermore, to those who, strangers to our religion, require of us that we take up arms for the common good and kill humans, we can make this reply: . . . How much more rightful is it (that) whenever others (who not being Christians) wage war, those (who are Christians) militate by . . . preserving their hands uncontaminated, fighting by their prayers to God for whosoever (enemy or ally) is justly waging the war . . . so that anything whatsoever that is contrary and adverse to those who act justly may be overthrown. Thus, as it is we indeed who, by our prayers, overthrow the evil spirits that stir up wars, impel to the violation of treaties, and disturb peace, of much greater benefit then are we to sovereigns (both enemy and ally) than those who seem to be wielding the weapons. But we (Christians) even fight for the emperor more than all others. Doubtless, we are not to militate under him even if he were to force us to do so; but we militate for him, when we gather together apart in piety camps by our prayers to God." (*Contra Celsum, VIII-73.*)

We Are Sons of Peace

"To those who inquire from whence we are and who our Leader might be, we answer: We come commissioned by the commands of Jesus to cast into ploughshares the swords which previously we used for waging wars and to inflict punishments; and we turn into sickles our spear with which previously we struck, being provoked. Nor do we any longer take up arms against any nation, nor do we learn to wage war, being made sons of peace by Jesus, who is the Leader we follow, having forsaken those leaders to whom our forefathers adhered and under whom we were 'strangers to the Testament.' (Eph. 2:12)." (*Contra Celsum, V*:33.)

ST. CLEMENT OF ALEXANDRIA (d. 217): He advocates to renounce even to the mere representation on emblems of "swords and weapons, for those who seek peace." (*Paedagogus Lib. III, Cap. XI*). All men alike, soldiers included, ought to mind the Words of Christ. "Man who is born for heavenly contemplation . . . we exhort to the recognition of God. . . . Whether you be a farm laborer, we tell you, cultivate the earth, but, cultivating the earth, mind God. Again, you that be held by a love for navigation, navigate, but adhering to the Heavenly Pilot. You, the knowledge (of Christ) has caught employed in the army, hear you the Emperor who signals unto you the just things. . . . Therefore as men now heavy with surfeiting and drunkenness, do turn to sobriety. . . ." (*Admonition to Heathens, Protrepticus, X*-100.)

ST. JUSTIN (d. 167): "We Christians who after we have learned by the Apostles of Jesus, how to serve God . . . and who were sunk in war and mutual slaughter . . . throughout the whole world, we have changed, each one, our warfare instruments, our swords into ploughshares, our spears into sickles." (*Dialogus cum Tryphone Judaeo, CX*)

"That we ought to be forbearing, ready to serve all men and without any part in enmity, the words spoken by Him are as follows: 'To him that striketh thee on the one cheek, offer also the other. And him that taketh away from thee thy cloak, forbid not to take thy coat also' (St. Luke 6:29) . . . 'And whosoever will force thee one mile, go with him other two' (St. Matt. 5:41). For it behooves not to answer fighting with fighting, nor does God wish us to be imitations of the harmful; but He has exhorted to lead all men away from wickedness and the cupidity of the harmful by forbearance and kindness." (*Apologia Prima XVI.*)

Conquer by Persuasion

"We who previously had the ways of money and possessions in preference to all, now, whatever we possess, we put together in common and we communicate with all the needy irrespectively; we who fought in mutual enmities and slaughters, now, after Christ has come . . . we pray for enemies; and those who pursue us with unjust enmities, we struggle to conquer them by persuasion." (*Apologia Prima XIV.*)

"When the Prophetic Spirit speaks as announcing the future, He speaks thus: 'For the Law shall come forth from Sion and the Word of the Lord from Jerusalem. And he shall judge the nations and rebuke many people: and they shall turn their swords into ploughshares and their spears into sickles. Nation shall not lift up sword against nation, neither shall they be exercised any more to war' (Is. 2:4). And it is possible to persuade you that it so happened.

"For, from Jerusalem, twelve men set out into the world and these, ignorant and not gifted with the faculty of speechmaking . . . and we who previously marched on to mutual slaughters, not only do we not wage war with the enemy, but also, lest we cheat or deceive those who cross-examine us, willingly we suffer death bearing witness to Christ. . . . But it would be ridiculous that those bound to you by an oath, and conscript soldiers, should prefer the fealty sworn to you—who can give them nothing incorruptible—to their own life, parents, homestead, and all things dear to them; and that we who thirst for uncorrupted life, should not forbear all things in order that we may attain our hopes from Him who can grant them." (*Apologia Prima XXXIX*: 1:5.)

Why Is There Strife?

POPE ST. CLEMENT I (d. 99): "Why is there strife and anger and disunion and war amongst you? Have we not one God, one Christ? Is not one Holy Spirit poured out on us?

Have we not one calling in Christ? Why do the Members of Christ tear one another? Why do we rise up against our own Body in such madness? Have we forgotten that we are all members of one another?" (Quoted in *The Catholic Worker*, Nov., 1940.)

To say nothing of St. Ignatius of Antioch (d. 107), St. Pachomius (d. 349), St. Telemachus, and last but not least Tertullian (d. 240), Athenagoras, Tatian, Lactantius (d. 325), Arnobius (d. 327), St. Jerome (d. 420), St. Paulin Nolan (d. 431) . . . recognized as uncompromising Pacifists.

The fact is that Christlike Pacifism was so general among Christians that the Church officials were able to enforce evangelical canons forbidding the use of deadly weapons.

Do Violence to No Man

THE APOSTOLIC CONSTITUTIONS, Book VIII: 32-10, declare that the soldier who presents himself for Baptism is to be instructed that he must do violence to no man, and be content with his hire. (St. Luke 3:14.) If he promise to observe this rule he is to be received; if he refuse he is to be rejected.

CANONICAL DECREES COMPILED BY (ST.) HYPPOLITUS (d. 235). Canon XI:9-11: "As for the soldier who is on duty, suffer him not to kill humans. . . . If, however, he is not willing, he must be rejected. If catechumens or any of the faithful want to become soldiers, let them be rejected." 13: "Soldiers (Christian) are not to kill even if this is commanded to them." 14: "The Christian is not to voluntarily become a soldier, if he is not coerced by a driver. He who bears the sword is to beware that he make no bloodshed. If he shed blood he is to abstain from participation in the mysteries. . . ."

THE GENERAL COUNCIL OF NICEA, A. D. 325: Canon XI: "If any, having been called by God's grace, have at first proven their faith by renouncing the army, but after this have returned to their own vomit, so as to . . . try and return to the army again, such as these are to be ten years among the penitents. . . ."

ECCLESIASTICAL REGULATIONS FOR EGYPT, Redaction 4th Century. Canon XI:9-11: "As for the soldier who is on duty, suffer him not to kill humans. If catechumens or faithful want to become soldiers, let them be rejected, for they have slighted God."

CANONICAL DECREES APPLIED BY ST. BASIL THE GREAT (d. 379). Canon XIII: "Our forefathers (pagan) have not held as murders the massacres committed at war; sparing, as it seems to me, those who fight for honor and love of country. However, it will be rightly advised that such as these, since their hands are not pure, abstain for three years from communion only."

POPE ST. LEO THE GREAT (d. 461): "It is altogether contrary to the regulations of the Church to return, after doing penance, to military service in the world, since the Apostle says that no soldier in God's service entangles himself in the affairs of the world."

Such canons have since been restricted to the clergy. Today, in some countries even the actual canons on military service are becoming obsolete; in France, for example.

Decrees Forbade War

It is worth noting that warfare, justified or not, was against positive ecclesiastical decrees, as eating meat on Fridays, for instance. The disciplinary regulations of the Church officials may change with the times as it is seen fit. For example, the practice of evangelic continence for the Western clergy was not always required, though always desired of all. But who would insinuate that a practice is evil and sinful after the Church officials have once not simply permitted and blessed it, as for the use of skis and motor cars, but positively prescribed it by canonical decrees?

It is worth noting also that Christians or even mere catechumens were not to become soldiers. They were not allowed to volunteer for the army after they had become soldiers of Christ. However, pagans already hired in the army could retain this means of earning their bodily needs and be received to baptism. This concession for the conversion of pagans is recognized even by Tertullian. "It is sought," he relates in his De Idolatria XIX, "whether a Christian can take up the military career, and the military career thus be admitted to the (Christian) Faith? . . . No career assigned to an illicit act is licit among Christians (apud nos)." Again in the De Corona XI: "It is a transgression to give one's name from the (Christian) camp of light to the (military) camp of darkness. The condition is plainly different if those already taken up in the army, the faith overtakes later on, as of those whom John the Baptist admitted to baptism (St. Lk. 3:14)—as of the most faithful centurions whom Christ approved (St. Matt. 8:10), and whom Peter catechized (Acts 10:44)—then, either it be withdrawing immediately as done by many, or cavilling by all means lest anything against God be committed. . . ."

Martyred Objectors Sainted

Many pagan soldiers, on becoming Christians, renounced their military employment, sometimes at the cost of martyrdom, for which some of them have been sainted. Many others were content to receive baptism without forsaking the army. The Rev. Victor White, O.P., notes that it is known from the celebrated letter of Marcus Aurelius to the Senate that there were already many Christian Legionaries by the time of the Legio fulminata, A. D. 174, and that even these manifested their hatred of armed force, and their preference for specifically Christlike and spiritual weapons. They flatly refused to kill humans and shed blood, even at the command of their military authorities. In this they were only faithful and loyal to the Christian ideal proposed to them by the canonical decrees of the Church officials.

Ignoring the texts, a jingoist might fancy that what was objectionable to Christians about the army was not bloodshed and the killing of humans, but solely the fact that soldiers were obliged to perform ceremonial acts of idolatry and to officially apostatize. But the decrees and regulations themselves are still on record for all who can read.

Furthermore, except, of course, for periods of persecution, even Tertullian in the De Idolatria, XIX, admits that there was "no necessity for idolatrous immolations" in the Militia Caligata, the Sandaled Army; that is, the career of the plain soldier and lower officers up to the grade of centurion exclusively (cfr. Marquardt). And so, without scruples, Tertullian tells the pagans: "We Christians do military service together with you." In patristics, however, the distinction between *bellare*, to wage war, and *militare*, to do military service, is always respected. The former all Christians, soldiers as well as others, ought to renounce; the latter was a concession for the Christian only if hired in the army before his catechism and baptism. Well, then, might the rational military strategist reasonably and naturally say: of what practicalness is a soldier if he may not kill humans or even shed blood?

Roman Army a Police Force

To quote the Rev. Victor White, O. P.: "The Roman Empire during the early days of the Christian era was not one state among many; her army was not an army among many. The Roman Empire was, it was supposed, the whole world—the *Orbis Romanus*. Correspondingly, the Roman Army was something essentially different from the army of a modern state. In theory, and to a considerable extent in practice, it was nearer to the modern idea of a police force than that of an army. . . . In a very real sense, the function of the army was to preserve peace; not in the sense of the modern politician of intimidating others into not making war, but in the very real sense of preserving from disruption the existing unity, the *tranquillitas ordinis*, of the whole world.

"In seeking precedents, therefore, from the thought and conduct of earlier Christians, we must be on our guard lest we use such terms as war, army, soldier, even patria, in a wholly different sense from that in which they could have understood it. For the early Christian (within the Empire) the question of international war between equal sovereign states simply did not arise, for it did not exist.

"His horror of war was a horror of the use of violence even for the maintenance of internal order and peace. Of the goodness of the end and of its claims upon the collaboration of Christians, he had no doubt. But he questioned the legitimacy and even the value of violence as a means for attaining that end. Even when . . . he would allow that non-Christians might legitimately fight, he would question whether Christians might join them." (War and the Early Church, in Blackfriars, Sept., 1939.)

BETHUNE

Death of Father Onesimus Lacouture, S. J.
by Dorothy Day
The Catholic Worker, December 1951

Fr. Onesimus Lacouture, S.J., was born in a little town north of Montreal, St. Ours, on April 13, 1881. He was the nineteenth child of his father, Xavier, who was married twice. His mother, Catherine, was his father's second wife. The first marriage brought forth ten children, the second eleven!

Doesn't that sound like the beginning of the life of a saint? Peter Maurin was one of twenty-three children. These two men who had the most influence on my life (and in a way on the life of the Catholic Worker) were both French peasants, of France and French Canada. They both knew the life of the land and the city. Both were men of the poor.

Fr. Lacouture lived only the first six years of his life in the village of St. Ours. Then the family moved to the mill town of Woonsocket, Rhode Island, where they lived a year and then moved to Ashland, and later to Cochituate, Massachusetts. Onesimus graduated from public high school in 1900 and went to the college of the Assumption near Montreal, and after two years to the novitiate of the Society of Jesus at Sault-aux-Recollets. It is there that he was buried last week, after a requiem mass in the chapel. He died on November 16, the feast of St. Gertrude, and was buried on November 20.

One of our dear friends notified me of his death, and I was able to take a bus to Montreal and attend the funeral. The last time I had seen Fr. Lacouture was at Sudbury, Canada, where I had gone to speak. He was procurator of the college there and we talked all one day of the spiritual life and of the retreats which we had been having since we met Father Pacifique Roy, another Canadian, in 1940, when he had introduced us to the work of Fr. Lacouture.

History

Fr. Lacouture's history briefly is this. After he left the novitiate he studied English at St. Andrew's on the Hudson in Poughkeepsie,

New York. Then he was sent back to Canada for three years of philosophy at the Jesuit Seminary in Montreal. Then according to the Jesuit plan of studies, he interrupted his studies for four years of teaching. For one year of this time, he taught Latin at the novitiate, then he was sent to Alaska to teach the Eskimos. He lived in the wilderness, in hardship and loneliness, and here he made two retreats by himself, out under the sky, in the great woods, reading and praying much as the Jesuit martyrs who where the first missionaries to the Indians did before him. Later he resumed his studies, and took his four years of theology in Montreal. He was ordained on the feast of St. Ignatius, 1916. He was then thirty-five and the first World War had been going on for two years. He volunteered for service as a military chaplain. His duties took him to France and with troop ships to India and on returning was demobilized in 1919. From England he went to Belgium where he made his tertianship, a third year of novitiate which Jesuits make after they are priests. One of his companions during this year was Fr. Raoul Plus, whose books we are all familiar with.

First Retreat

When he returned he became prefect of St. Boniface's College in Manitoba for three years, then he went to Caughnawaga, near Montreal, where he was for four years pastor of that Indian Mission. This is the shrine of Katari Tekakwitha where he began to give his now famous conferences on the spiritual life. They aroused such enthusiasm that his superior put him on the Mission Band, which had its headquarters at the novitiate at Sault-aux-Recollets.

The first retreat given to priests began on Father Lacouture's fiftieth birthday in 1931, and the last was in 1939. In those eight years he had given 142 retreats to 6,089 priests. When his retreat work was stopped he spent some time at Santa Barbara, California, at Loyola University in Los Angeles, at Edmonton College, Alberta, and finally at St. Regis Mission, on the border of Canada and New York, where he died. At the time I saw him, he was serving briefly at the college at Sudbury from which he returned to St. Regis.

Sudden Death

He had been in excellent health when on Thursday night, November 15, he had a sudden stroke. After an hour of consciousness during which time he was anointed and received Extreme Unction, he became unconscious and died the next morning while his superior was offering up the Sacrifice of the Mass. He had been taken to the hospital at Cornwall, Ontario, which was the nearest hospital.

A solemn requiem Mass was sung at St. Regis and Bishop Langlois of Valleyfield sang the *Libera me*. Then the body was brought to Montreal, thirty cars full of Indians driving after the hearse for eight miles.

Fr. Lacouture's relatives from Brockton, Providence and Boston came to the funeral, his own superior, Fr. Lalonde, and some of his former associates. I was the only one who arrived from the States.

"It was a very small funeral, considering how great a man Fr. Lacouture was," one of his friends said. "Just a few years ago he was famous. Now he is anonymous."

"Unless the seed fall into the ground and die, itself remaineth alone. But if it die it beareth much fruit."

The Doctrine

The Catholic Worker group first heard of the famous retreat which caused so much controversy in 1940 when our friend, Sister Peter Claver, brought Fr. Pacifique Roy to see us on Mott street. Fr. Roy began immediately giving us *the doctrine,* as he always called it, and it was indeed a glowing and a beautiful thing. Fr. Roy sat down to the breakfast table with us that morning, and began talking of the love of God, how by our baptism we had been made the sons of God and what that entailed for us, what responsibilities it laid upon us. We had to put off the old man and put on the new, we had to die to ourselves and rise with Christ and death was painful, indeed a terrible thing. "It is terrible thing to fall into the hands of a living God!" This salvation of ours was a life and death matter. It had cost our Lord His life on the Cross. We are bought with a great price.

We began to recognize our worth as we heard such talk. We began to recognize our responsibilities. It was the kind of retreat which could be preached to the men on the breadline, to the worker, the scholar, to young and old, the educated and uneducated. It was the good news!

Wept for Joy

Father Roy knew the retreat by heart, since he had made it about ten times. He could repeat conferences word for word, and he did so with a warm and happy earnestness. He liked to tell how people received the retreat, how "they wept for joy." May of the young priests who made the retreat under Fr. Lacouture, and in turn gave it to us, used to like to gloat over the difficulties of it. Sometimes I thought they were rubbing it in.

There were four or five conferences a day, of an hour each. Sometimes the too enthusiastic ones ran over the hour. Afterwards there was a fifteen-minutes period of meditation in the chapel before the Blessed Sacrament. Complete silence was maintained for a week. There could be no time for writing letters, reading books. Only the New Testament or the psalms were allowed. If you put yourself in the hands of the retreat master you had to follow directions, as though you were in the care of a physician, and indeed Fr. Lacouture was a physician of souls.

Oakmount

When we first heard of the retreats and began making them they were given at Oakmount, Pa., where Father Farina was chaplain of a small orphanage. The retreats were held during the summer, every two weeks, and the Sisters, Zelatrice of the Sacred Heart, were only too happy to make up dormitories in the classrooms and feed us delightful Italian meals. We wrote about these retreats in *The Catholic Worker*, and many were the readers of the paper who came to make them. Many a young priest who had made the retreat himself either under Fr. Lacouture or under Father John J. Hugo, sent their friends, parishioners, and sometimes non-Catholics, to hear this good news.

Applied Christianity

The retreats were supposedly for men and women separately, but always there were men who could not get to their own retreat, and women who had to go to the men's retreat, and priests who wanted to get in on it (even Monsignori) so the retreats were mixed, indeed. Agnostic Jews, practicing Protestants, Quakers and Catholics, all made it. Fr. Hugo, Fr. Meenan, Fr. Corcoran, Fr. Farina, these were some of those who gave conferences, that were so alive, so glowing, that we will never forget them. And all of these conferences, followed quite literally a pattern laid down by Fr. Lacouture, a course of teaching which did not vary. Fr. Hugo's *Applied Christianity* were, as he points out, the retreat notes of Fr. Lacouture, perhaps embellished by illustration and allusion to other spiritual writers, corroborating the points made.

The Stuff

What was it that we were so taken with in the retreat? Of course it was stimulating, glowing, alive, challenging. We none of us laymen made it under Fr. Lacouture, but most of the retreat masters we heard were good teachers, though some irritated by mannerisms or by faults of temperament. But it was the stuff! It was the stuff of life, of eternal life.

For one thing, it was what Peter Maurin taught, but he spoke of the life of this world. There was no saying, "what can I do about it? What responsibility is it of mine?" Both men recognized the dignity of the laity, the capacity of the laymen for sacrifice, for sanctity. Both recognized indeed, that without sanctity it was impossible to see God!

For too long, too little had been expected of us. When Christ spoke, he spoke from the Mount to the multitudes. He called on all men to take up their cross and follow Him. When we listened to Fr. Lacouture's retreat, we began to understand the distinction between nature and the supernatural (we understand that grace builds on nature and we saw for the first time man's spiritual capacities raised as he is to be a child of God. We saw the basis of our dignity.

Courage

I could write a great deal about that retreat, and all it brought to us, the new vistas which opened out before us. But I will simply say that it gave us spiritual direction. We were learning how to die to ourselves, to live in Christ, and all the turmoil of the movement, all the pruning of natural love, all the disappointments were explained by the doctrine of the Cross. The retreat gave us hope and courage, as retreats are supposed to do, and we will be everlastingly grateful for it, grateful to Fr. Laouture, who made the retreat possible for us. We feel that we have been participants in a great spiritual movement which is still going on, though it is perhaps now in shadow. The seed has fallen into the ground and has died. But we know that it will bear great fruit.

Misunderstanding

This Onesimus was like the obedient slave of the New Testament. But his master did not free him. After the retreats were stopped because of increasing misunderstandings and controversies, Fr. Onesimus Lacouture lived in silence and solitude with the Iroquois Indians on a mission only eighty miles from Montreal but hard of access. He offered the Holy Sacrifice of the Mass each day, but he no longer preached or taught. He accepted his situation gaily, with joy, rejoicing in tribulation, feeling that he was following the pattern which has been set through the ages. We can say little about the controversy but we do know that he has suffered at the hands of over-zealous friends as well as at the hands of his opponents. We hope and trust that his writings, his lucid and clear and glowing presentation of the spiritual life will see the light of day, and that after his writings are examined they will be given to the public.

I should like to see his on gravestone the words, "He made all things new," because his teaching of the love of God so aroused our love in turn, that a sense of the sacramentality of life was restored for us, and a new vigor and meaning was given to our lives. "He made all things new."

P.S. All of the priests who gave this retreat are stationed in parishes and hard at work teaching and preaching and dispensing the sacraments. Fr. Hugo is at Butler. Pa., Fr. Farina is at Donora, Pa., Fr. Corcoran died of cancer, but all the other young priests who shared in this work are most active in their work for souls. There has been no condemnation of the ideas of the retreat although the retreat itself was stopped.

Applied Christianity has the Imprimatur of the archdiocese of New York.[1]

[1] Soon to be available from Loreto Publications.